LANTERN LANE

BOOK 3

WRITTEN BY
TESSA GREENE

COVER ILLUSTRATION BY
KRISTINA KISTER

COVER DESIGN BY
PHILLIP COLHOUER

TABLE OF CONTENTS

CHAPTER 1

Letty stood in the doorway of the cold, empty dungeon that was illuminated by nothing more than a bit of sunlight trickling through a small, narrow opening high in the wall. The pale light landed on two men sitting against the wall, huddled in thin, ratty blankets. One of them Letty had expected to see—in fact, her suspicion that he was here had driven her down to the dungeon in the first place. She instantly recognized him as Rylan the cobbler, who had disappeared from Lantern Lane about a week before.

Who Letty hadn't expected to see was the man sitting next to Rylan. His tight blond curls and green eyes, his broad shoulders and strong frame—although thinner than she remembered—were all very familiar to her.

"Papa?" she asked as tears sprang to her eyes.

Papa squinted, and then his eyes widened to the size of saucers. His jaw slackened. After a moment of staring in shock, he stumbled to his feet and took a few staggering steps forward.

"Letty, my girl? Is that you?" His voice was raspy and strained.

"What are you doing here?" Letty's lip trembled as she spoke, and the tears pooling in her eyes began to fall. She'd thought her father was dead. *Everyone* thought her father was dead! How had he ended up in the palace dungeon without anyone knowing?

"That doesn't matter; don't talk about that," Papa hushed. He carefully pulled her into his familiar and comforting embrace, and Letty never wanted him to let go. She could feel his body shaking, and the soft sound of his sniffling accompanied the droplets falling onto her hair. She sobbed into his shoulder as he whispered, "My girl. My sweet, darling girl."

"Everyone thinks you died," Letty whimpered. "I missed you so, so much."

"I know, Letty. I'm sorry."

They stood there, relishing each other's presence again. After a moment, Papa pushed her away from him and wiped a few tears from her cheeks. "Now, tell me what you did to your arm. Is it broken?"

Shaking her head and giggling, Letty said, "I'm just clumsy, Papa. I fell and strained it. It'll heal up fast." She stepped away from him so she could see his eyes as she asked, "Was it actually you? That night I was in the garden. Miles told me the search parties had given up, and we assumed you died." Letty glanced up at the narrow opening and realized that the leaves and flowers she could see belonged to the winter rose bush. "You saw me through the window and spoke to me, didn't you?"

Tears continued to stream down Papa's face. "I did. I shouldn't have. I'm sure it was confusing for you, and I'm sorry for that. I just couldn't help myself when I heard you crying. The hardest thing for parents is to watch their children suffer." His voice broke.

"But why didn't you answer me again when I called for you? Why didn't you tell me that you were here and that you were all right?" Her tears became hotter now as anger started to edge its way in. "I needed you, and you didn't answer me even though you heard."

"There, there, my dear. I know that must have hurt. I wanted more than anything to comfort you, but I couldn't say more. It would have put you in terrible danger, and I couldn't do that to my little girl."

"Danger? What danger?"

Papa shook his head. "Please don't ask for details. The less you know, the safer you'll be. It's the only way I can protect my family right now."

"But that doesn't make any sense! You're not a criminal, Papa, so why are you here? And what is the danger?"

The guard, Clement, pushed the door slightly open and stuck his head into the room. "All right, visiting time is over. You have to go," he said to Letty.

"I'm not ready yet," Letty replied, a pleading tone making its way into her voice.

"Look, you shouldn't be here to begin with. It's time to go."

"He's right, Letty," Papa said. "I don't know how you found out I was here, but it's best that you leave."

"But Papa—"

"Please, Letty, trust me," he begged, gazing deeply into her eyes. Reluctantly, she nodded. "Can I have one more hug before you go? I have missed you so." He held his arms out, and the tenderness in his eyes made her want to weep again.

Letty wrapped her arm around her papa's waist, squeezing him as tightly as she could.

"I love you, Papa," she whispered. "And I'll be back, I promise."

"Letty—" he began, but he was interrupted by Rylan.

"I'm sorry, but I have to know if my family is all right. Have you seen them, Letty?" Rylan asked. "I'm worried about Kiana taking care of the children all alone."

Turning from Papa's arms, Letty looked at Rylan. "I saw them a few days ago. They're okay, don't worry. Our neighbors are taking care of them," she assured him. "But I'm sure they will be so relieved to know you're all right."

"No, Letty, you can't tell his family," Papa said firmly, "or ours, for that matter. No one can know that either of us is here."

"But why?"

Clement rapped his fist against the door frame again. "Really, it's time to go," he insisted.

"Just trust me," Papa repeated emphatically. "Now go. I love you, my girl."

Frustration simmered in Letty's chest. She didn't understand, but the impatient tapping of Clement's boot against the cold stone floor told her that there was no use begging for more time. Letty inhaled deeply, squared her shoulders, and turned on her heel, fighting to keep her lip from quivering again. Clement closed and locked the door firmly behind her, once again trapping Rylan and Papa in their dungeon cell.

"The blond man—he's your father?" Clement asked, shifting uncomfortably.

"Yes," Letty replied, then lowered her voice. "Clement, please tell me why he's here. My father has never done anything illegal." She had overheard King Henrick tell King Dorian of Pelorias that one of the prisoners in the dungeon—Rylan the cobbler, based on

King Henrick's description—was there for something to do with treasonous information. She added, "And he isn't a traitor. So how did he end up here?"

"I couldn't tell you if I wanted to," Clement responded, unconcerned.

"But you *have* to know!"

Clement shrugged. "I'm not the one who arrested him, kid. I have no idea what charges either of them is being held on. I'm just following my orders, and if you don't leave, I'm going to be dismissed from my position."

Letty's shoulders slumped. Everything about this situation was maddening, and she could feel a headache coming on from the confusion and frustration of the past few minutes. She couldn't ignore Papa's warnings about safety; he had always protected her, and she trusted him enough to know that if he was concerned, there was a good reason for it. She only wished she knew the reason! She would usually discuss something like this with her brother, Miles, but Papa had specifically said that no one else in her family could know.

"I'm going to make sure there's no one outside before you leave," Clement informed her. He climbed the stairs, keeping an eye on both Letty and the prison door as he did. He poked his head up through the cellar door and looked around for a few seconds. When he was done, he pulled his head back inside and beckoned for Letty to come. "I'll help you lift the door," he said when she arrived at the top of the steps.

Letty nodded. "Thank you for your help, Clement," she said. "I appreciate it."

Clement didn't reply but gave one firm nod before pushing the door upward. Letty scurried out of the opening as quickly as she could. Although her heart was racing, she steadied her pace as she broke through the trees as though nothing had happened at all.

CHAPTER 2

L etty, what do you think of Prince Cassius?" Princess Maisy asked as Letty struggled with the many laces of the princess's evening gown. Since receiving a sling from the doctor, Letty had to position herself awkwardly to get any use out of her right hand, but she managed to pull the final lace into place.

Fluffing the many-tiered layers of the skirt, Letty considered how to answer. Honestly, she didn't *know* what she thought about the prince. So far, he had failed to impress her, but then again, she had only interacted with him for a few minutes, and during their last interaction, she had been too distracted by the anticipation of visiting the dungeon to give him any consideration at all. In fact, it took a great deal of effort to pay full attention during the conversation she was having now, a few hours after returning.

"I'm not sure," Letty replied at last, erring on the side of caution. "The more important question is, what do *you* think of him?"

Princess Maisy shrugged softly, causing her puffed sleeves to rustle. "He's the prince. What more is there to say beyond that?"

Letty stood up straight, put her hand on her hip, and looked Princess Maisy straight in the eye. "I should think you'd have something more to say, considering that you asked the question to begin with."

"No," Princess Maisy said with a shake of her head. "He's just not what I expected."

"How so?" Letty placed her hand on Princess Maisy's elbow and guided her over to the vanity, where she sat the princess down.

"Well . . . he reminds me a great deal of myself from before you started helping me, not the version of me I like best," the princess confided, staring in the mirror as Letty positioned herself carefully behind her. With a skillful adjustment of her injured arm, Letty began twisting the dark hair into a simple, elegant chignon.

"What do you mean?"

"He doesn't seem to care much about other people. And I know I'm not perfect—only a few days ago, I was just as selfish, maybe more so. But I don't want to be that person anymore, and I am trying so hard to change. Maybe he could, too, but I can't imagine marrying him unless he does."

Letty was fascinated to hear some of these innermost thoughts. She had never thought much about courtship herself—she felt that fourteen was still too young for that—beyond teasing her older brother a bit. Still, she wanted to help Princess Maisy as best she could.

"Why do you think he doesn't care about other people?" Letty asked, hoping to gain a better understanding of what was really causing the princess doubt.

"Well, you heard him call you 'girl' at tea—just like I used to do—and he didn't seem to care when I corrected him. Plus, at the piano earlier today, he didn't care to listen; all he wanted to do was show off. That's how it was all day."

"I see," Letty said. "I think you're right to pay attention to the way he treats people, and if you don't like it, that's something that should cause you to hesitate. But may I give you a suggestion before you jump to a conclusion?"

"Please, do."

"I have to wonder if there's another reason he's behaving this way right now. Maybe he's just nervous to be around you, or he doesn't understand the type of manners you expect. Maybe you're right and that's just the way he is; who knows? But if I were you, I think I would give him another chance before you make any decisions—he will be here for another two days, after all."

In the mirror Letty could see the princess's gaze shift to stare into the distance as she considered her words. "That makes sense," she said. "Although I wouldn't say there's much of a decision to be made."

Letty's eyebrows scrunched together. "What do you mean? Of course there's a decision."

Princess Maisy shook her head, and Letty narrowly avoided poking the princess's scalp with a hairpin. "If the prince proposes to me, I am expected to accept. My uncle has made that very clear," she said.

"But surely you can say no if you want to. You *are* the one being betrothed, after all."

"I know, but I'm also a princess, and I have responsibilities."

Letty didn't answer. She didn't know what to say. She couldn't imagine what it would be like to live a life where her own wishes and desires were not respected or even considered.

Princess Maisy sighed. "Enough about that. How was your afternoon?"

"It was . . . all right," Letty said. Could she tell the princess about her escapade a few hours before? Clement had made it sound as though she could be in massive trouble if the king—or perhaps anyone—found out she had gone to the dungeon. Then again, Princess Maisy had been so understanding with everything Letty told her about her father up to that point, and since the princess had just been vulnerable with Letty about her feelings, Letty felt a bit more confident. Plus, Princess Maisy might even know something that would help.

Letty inhaled deeply through her nose. "Actually, there's something I want to talk to you about. Could we do that tonight, maybe while you're getting ready for bed?"

Princess Maisy's forehead creased as her eyebrows came together. "Are you sure it isn't something you want to discuss right now? Is everything all right?"

"Don't worry about it now," Letty assured her. Although, if it weren't for the prince visiting, she would have loved to have it all out then and there. "Enjoy the evening with your visitors, and we'll talk afterward, if you're still willing."

Princess Maisy nodded solemnly, concern evident on her face. "Of course. I'll be ready," she said. The princess's head swiveled toward the clock on the wall. "Oh, goodness, I have to get to supper. I'm almost late."

Letty stuck one final pin through Princess Maisy's hair and replaced the crown on top of her head, admiring the way it sparkled in the dull light. "I'm finished. You're ready to go," she said.

"Thank you, Letty!" Princess Maisy gathered her long, layered skirt with the swoop of a hand so she could move more quickly, using her other hand to keep her crown in place as she ran, gracefully as always, out of her bedroom.

Letty waited a few moments before making her way down the stairs, just in case the prince or his parents were waiting for Princess Maisy. She wasn't sure how to interact with all these royals who did not seem nearly as comfortable having her around as Princess Maisy was, so if there was a simple way to avoid an awkward encounter, she would take it.

When Letty at last arrived in the kitchen, she found the entire kitchen staff slumped on tables and countertops, draped over the backs of their chairs, or leaning heavily against the walls—a surprising contrast from the normal chaotic energy that reigned in the kitchen.

"Is everyone okay?" Letty asked as her eyes darted about, nervously examining the exhausted faces of the kitchen staff.

Soft chuckles rippled through the kitchen. A few of the kitchen hands peeled themselves off the surfaces they were resting on.

"We're fine," one of the cooks laughed. "Their supper is on the table now, and dessert is ready to go out whenever King Henrick asks for it. We're just a bit tuckered out from preparing it all," she explained.

"Oh, you poor things," Letty said. "Well, it smells wonderful in here. You all need to eat now, too, and get your energy back up."

"She's right," a kitchen hand agreed. "I'm starved."

Everyone else nodded and murmured in agreement, then set about laying out the remaining pheasant, boiled potatoes, and roasted vegetables that had not been served to the royalty in the other room.

Jocelyn trudged into the kitchen right as everyone began to queue for their supper. Dirt smudged her face and hands, and the brown, wet spots on her knees looked as though she had been kneeling in soil.

"What happened to you?" Letty asked, completely taken aback.

Jocelyn sighed and wiped the back of her hand across her forehead, adding another streak of grime to the collection on her face. "Apparently, Prince Cassius had some opinions about the gardens and all the things that were wrong with them, so the gardeners needed help digging things up and moving them around."

Hmm, Letty thought, *maybe my theory about him just being nervous was wrong.*

Letty followed as Jocelyn trudged over to the washbasin, poured water over her hands, and vigorously scrubbed every bit of grime away. Letty quickly found a clean rag and wet it so Jocelyn could remove the dirt from her face before getting in line for the meal.

They didn't speak much as they made their way through the queue—they were too focused on loading their plates with the steaming offerings. Letty was famished, and she assumed Jocelyn was, too, after working so hard in the gardens.

Once they were both seated at the kitchen table with napkins in their laps, Jocelyn casually asked, "Have you ever seen that little window right next to the ground in the gardens?"

Letty's eyebrows arched, and she stopped in the middle of cutting a piece of pheasant. "Yes," Letty replied slowly. "Why?"

"Well, I noticed it while I was tending the garden, and I thought about what you mentioned earlier today—you know, all that about dungeons and such. I just thought that maybe, if you really are as determined as you seem to see if your neighbor is there, you could check through that window. I would imagine it must go to the dungeon."

It was all Letty could do to restrain herself from laughing. Jocelyn's observation was, at this point, about as helpful as the call from a cuckoo clock running hours behind. Still, Letty decided that this was a good opportunity to invite Jocelyn to hear the rest of what she had learned about the dungeon that day.

"Jocelyn, would you come up to Princess Maisy's bedroom while she gets ready for bed tonight?" Letty asked.

Jocelyn's nose crinkled. "Why?"

"There's something I'd like to talk to you both about. I need your advice," Letty explained. "I'll make sure the princess is all right with having you join us first, of course."

Jocelyn eyed Letty suspiciously as she went back to her supper. "All right," she agreed. "I'll meet you later tonight."

This talk of the dungeon made Letty wonder how Rylan and Papa were faring. They had both looked much thinner than they usually were, and Jocelyn's reminder of the window had given Letty an idea. She shoved a few more bites of food into her mouth, then slipped the rest of her pheasant, potatoes, and vegetables into the napkin in her lap as Jocelyn watched, clearly wondering what in the world was going on.

"I've got to go," Letty said, tying her napkin into a small bundle with the food in the center. "I'll be back soon."

"Oh, uh . . . okay," Letty heard Jocelyn say, but she was halfway out of the kitchen before Jocelyn could ask why.

Letty slipped out the front doors as silently and casually as she could, nodding with a pleasant smile at the guards as she passed them. "Just running a quick errand," she explained to one who looked confused about why she would leave in the middle of suppertime.

She made her way around the corner of the palace, through the garden, and to the window opening by the winter rose bush. She crouched down, slid her bundle of food through the bars, and dropped it to the ground.

"I love you, Papa," she whispered into the dungeon below.

Her father's figure appeared directly below the opening so she could see most of his face. He dropped out of view for a moment as he bent down to pick up her gift from the floor. When he stood, he held one finger to his lips. "Don't get caught here," he said as quietly as he could while still being heard. Then he kissed the finger against his lips and held it up in Letty's direction. "I love you, too."

Letty grinned and, with that, ran back to the palace to rejoin Jocelyn for the remainder of supper.

CHAPTER 3

Ll right, Letty, what's going on? I've been worrying all night!"
Princess Maisy exclaimed. She had just finished her evening
bath and was sitting on the chair next to her vanity in her cozy
pink nightgown, waiting to hear what Letty had to say.

Letty had spent the princess's entire bath time pacing the floor,
wondering how to have this conversation. She had already asked
Princess Maisy and Jocelyn to talk tonight, and she still wanted to,
but the closer it got, the more butterflies gathered in her stomach,
fluttering around as though they were looking for an escape route.

"Would it be all right if we wait for Jocelyn?" Letty asked. "I'd
really like to get advice from both of you on this, if you don't mind
her being here."

"That's fine. We can wait," Princess Maisy said. She fidgeted
with the hairbrush sitting on the vanity, flipping it over and over as
she waited. Letty started picking at her fingers, paying attention to
her breathing and trying to make sure she didn't get too panicky
before she could even speak.

It wasn't long before Jocelyn announced herself with a knock at
the door. "Okay, Letty, what's going on? I've been waiting to hear
for hours," she said, moving into the room as Letty opened the
door for her.

"Me, too," Princess Maisy agreed. "What is on your mind?"

Letty inhaled deeply through her nose, then let out a huge puff of air. Was she *sure* this wouldn't go up in flames? She *couldn't* be sure, but she needed advice, and she couldn't turn to Mama or Miles this time. There was only one way to find out how this would go.

"I found my papa," Letty said at last. The words rushed out of her like water from a burst dam.

Jocelyn's and Princess Maisy's mouths gaped open, their eyes wide with surprise.

"Say that again, Letty. I don't think I heard you right," Jocelyn said.

Letty breathed out shakily, almost laughing as her eyes filled with tears. "I found Papa," she restated. She relished the way the words felt coming out of her mouth. The time he had been missing had felt so long—so long to be without hope. Now that she was saying it out loud, it felt like she was proving to reality itself that it was true.

"That's wonderful," Princess Maisy gushed. "Where in the world did you find him? And when? You've been here all day!"

"You're right," Letty said, "and that's the trouble. You see, I actually found him here. He's in the dungeon with a cobbler from Lantern Lane."

Princess Maisy's nose crinkled. "In *our* dungeon?" she asked. "I had no idea we had prisoners there right now. How unusual."

"Why is he in the dungeon?" Jocelyn asked incredulously. "From what you've told me about him, he sounds like a wonderful man."

"I don't know," Letty told Jocelyn. "Even the guard didn't seem to have any idea. Papa knew, obviously, but he refused to tell me. He said it was too dangerous." She turned to Princess Maisy and added, "I was hoping you could tell me what might have happened, Your Highness."

Princess Maisy shook her head slowly. "I haven't got a clue," she replied. "The dungeon doesn't typically get much use. Trielle is a very safe kingdom, and most criminals end up in a prison somewhere far away, near Alria. I heard there were prisoners there right now being held for treason, I think, but I hadn't heard anything about prisoners in the dungeon."

"Yes, treason—that's what King Henrick said the cobbler was imprisoned for, so maybe Papa was, too. But what does that entail?"

"Wait a moment! My uncle told you about the cobbler?" Princess Maisy asked, shocked. She raised one hand to her temple but motioned Letty to continue. "Start from the beginning," she instructed. "How did you actually find your father?"

"Well, it was really an accident, and I told Jocelyn the first part already." Letty shifted uncomfortably as she spoke, worried about how the princess would react. "I was cleaning up that map we left out in the library when I heard King Henrick and King Dorian coming. I got nervous, and I hid. Then, when they came in, King Henrick started talking about a prisoner in the dungeon, and I noticed that it sounded very much like a man who lives on my street who went missing awhile after my father did. The part I haven't told Jocelyn yet," she said, glancing at Jocelyn from the corner of her eye while she continued to speak to the princess, "is that I convinced one of the guards to let me inside."

Princess Maisy leaned back in her chair, an amused smirk on her face.

"Really, Letty?" Jocelyn scolded. "Even after you agreed that it was a bad idea?"

"I know. I'm sorry, but I saw a guard on the way out, and he agreed to bring me to the dungeon this afternoon. I just needed to know for sure if the cobbler was there. His wife and children are friends of mine, and they are so worried."

"Well, it worked out, didn't it?" Princess Maisy said to Jocelyn, dismissing her reprimand. "Go on, Letty. What happened next?"

"The guard told me where to meet him, so I went there after tea. He let me into the dungeon, and I was right! Rylan—he's the cobbler I was talking about—was right there. And Papa was sitting next to him." Letty skimmed her index finger beneath her eye to wipe away the moisture that had pooled there.

"Did you get to talk to him?" Jocelyn whispered, placing a hand on Letty's shoulder.

Letty nodded, then shook her head. "Not for long," she said. "Cl—" she caught herself before she said Clement's name. If she got in trouble, she didn't want to drag Clement down with her. "The *guard*," she corrected, "was worried that we would both get in trouble if I stayed."

"That's so strange," Princess Maisy murmured. She stood up and started pacing back and forth across her bedroom floor. "Most of the time, prisoners are allowed to have visitors. My government and diplomacy tutor talks about that all the time. No guard should be that worried about letting a prisoner see someone unless there is a specific reason." Princess Maisy paused her pacing for a moment to look at Letty. "Did the guard say *anything* about why he was so concerned?"

"Not really," Letty said, racking her brain. "Only that he was under the king's orders."

Princess Maisy's face twisted in confusion. "This is just so strange," she mused again. "I honestly don't know that I've ever heard of anything like this before. I just don't understand the secrecy . . ."

"You're not angry, Your Highness?" Letty asked. Now that the story was out and the princess had all the details, Letty needed to know if she had been in the wrong after all.

"No, of course not. I'm so glad you found your father—if he's one of our prisoners, you should have known where he was from the start." She lowered her voice slightly. "But we should do our best to make sure my uncle doesn't find out we know just yet. I don't know what's going on, but if he's trying to keep something secret, I'm not sure how he would react to our finding it out."

Letty nodded in agreement. She had no intention of confronting the king about her discovery. She would use any other means she could to investigate what was going on before she asked him about it.

"Are you going to tell your family, though? Your mother and brother?" Princess Maisy continued.

"I . . . don't know. I want to. They would be thrilled to know that Papa's alive and close by, and if I could, I would run home now and tell them. But Papa was insistent that they couldn't know. He said it was too dangerous, and for now, until I have more information, I just have to trust him."

"I'll do whatever I can to help you figure this out, Letty," Jocelyn promised.

"I will, too," Princess Maisy agreed. "In the meantime, if there is anything those men need—more blankets, extra food, anything— let me know, and I will arrange for them to have it." She paused for a moment, and a grin played at the corners of her mouth. "In fact, perhaps I will arrange for you to deliver it to them."

Letty gazed at the princess with admiration. "Thank you," she whispered. Just then, the clock on the wall chimed ten o'clock. "Oh, goodness, Your Highness, you should have been asleep half an hour ago." Letty jumped up from the edge of the princess's bed. "Thank you both for talking with me."

"Of course," Jocelyn replied.

"Thank *you*, Letty," Princess Maisy said. "I don't think anyone has ever confided in me before. It's nice." She shifted her weight from one foot to the other, looking a little apprehensive. "I feel as if I should give you a hug. Is that all right?" Immediately, she started backtracking. "If you don't want me to, that's perfectly fine; I just thought I'd see if—"

Letty interrupted the princess's rambling by throwing her arm around the princess's shoulders, trying to keep her other bound arm out of the way. Princess Maisy put her arms slowly and loosely around Letty's waist. Letty had never experienced a more awkward hug, but her heart was bursting that Princess Maisy had even offered.

"Well," Princess Maisy said abruptly, straightening out her nightgown after she and Letty broke their embrace. "You are free to go."

Letty laughed lightly and said good night to the princess and Jocelyn, then made her way down the hall to her own bedroom, suddenly exhausted. She got ready for bed as quickly as she could, then slipped between her soft, cream-colored sheets, sinking into the gentle warmth of her bed. The palace was still and quiet around her, and the room was peaceful and dark, illuminated only by the soft orange glow of the candle by her bedside. Letty blew out the candle's flame and tried to drift off to sleep.

Tired as she was, though, Letty lay awake, staring up at the ceiling as thoughts whirled through her mind. She was sure that Papa wasn't as warm and comfortable as she was. Maybe he was still awake, too, staring at grimy stone walls instead of cozy periwinkle-and-cream decor and huddling under a thin blanket instead of a plush comforter.

It really was odd, as Princess Maisy had said, that there was so much secrecy around Papa and Rylan's imprisonment. What could have possibly happened that needed so desperately to be hidden?

Come to think of it, many odd things had happened over the last few days. Besides the secrecy surrounding the prisoners, there had been Princess Maisy's confusion about the incorrect borders on the map in the library. Letty also couldn't forget the strange encounters between the king and the tall, curious visitor she had spied from the guest room. She couldn't make sense of any of it. These unusual events all laid themselves out like mixed-up puzzle pieces in Letty's mind. They seemed random and disconnected, yet she couldn't help but wonder if somehow they all fit together.

CHAPTER 4

The kitchen was in a state of hullabaloo the next morning with the usual chaos of preparing and serving breakfast combined with the last-minute groceries being delivered for the ball the next day. Mounds of unwashed fresh fruit covered the tables where the castle staff usually ate their breakfast, and blocks of butter and cheese were piled on the countertops, waiting to be used in pastries and hors d'oeuvres. A symphony of scents collided in the air: the sweet fragrance of the fruits, the savory potatoes and eggs being fried, and the spicy cinnamon from the oatmeal bubbling in a huge pot over the fire.

"Not much space to sit today, sorry," one of the cooks said as she handed Letty a steaming bowl of oatmeal topped with berries.

"That's all right. I don't have much time this morning, anyway," Letty replied. She found a tiny corner of empty counter space and set her bowl down.

"Oh? Does the princess have a special assignment for you before the ball tomorrow?"

Letty laughed. "No, no," she explained, "she and Prince Cassius are walking through Lantern Lane and some of the nearby villages today—you know, sort of a tour of the kingdom, or at least part of it. She asked if I would come with them since I live on Lantern

Lane and could show them things they might not see otherwise."

"A full morning walking around the kingdom with the prince and princess?" The cook chuckled sarcastically. "Have fun!"

Letty shrugged that comment away. She knew that it would probably be an uncomfortable interaction, just as every encounter with the prince had been thus far, but Princess Maisy had asked her to come along. Besides, it would be nice to get out of the castle for a while.

Letty slowly squished each juicy blueberry between her teeth as she ate her oatmeal, enjoying the tart and sweet bursts of flavor. After she scraped the last spoonful of oats out of the bottom of her bowl, she deposited the bowl in the washbasin and hurried up the stairs for her shawl. She glanced at the clock as she draped the shawl over her shoulders: 9:01 a.m. Princess Maisy would be finishing breakfast any minute now, and she and Letty had agreed earlier that morning that they would begin their little tour as soon as possible. Letty had even dressed the princess in traveling clothes instead of one of the gowns the seamstress had designed so that she could enjoy the long walk without worrying about dirtying her nice dress.

After one last glance around to make sure she wasn't forgetting anything, Letty started for the grand entry to wait for the prince and princess.

Before she could make it there, however, Princess Maisy came storming down the hallway. It looked to Letty as though the princess was biting the inside of her cheek, and her eyes were brimming with hot tears that she tried to blink away.

"Your Highness, what happened? Are you all right?"

"I'm fine," Princess Maisy snapped. She stopped herself, closed her eyes, and let out a shaky breath. "I'm fine," she repeated, softer now. "My uncle said I have to change before we go for our tour." She began walking more calmly now toward her room, and Letty fell in step behind her.

"Why? You're dressed perfectly for a good walk," Letty said. It was true: Princess Maisy's white dress was speckled with tiny purple floral print and was made of a thick cotton that would keep her warm in the late autumn weather.

"I thought so, too, but my uncle pulled me aside and was furious that I wasn't wearing one of the new dresses the seamstress designed. He said I was going to ruin my chances with the prince if I cared so little for how I looked."

Letty's fist clenched in its sling, and her shoulders tensed. "How could he say something like that?" Letty fumed. "You look beautiful in that dress, and besides, it's practical. Even if it were hideous, one ugly outfit wouldn't ruin a betrothal."

Princess Maisy sighed. "I wish you could tell my uncle that."

With a huff, the princess threw open her armoire doors and grabbed her buttercup-yellow dress from its hanger. "Prince Cassius is waiting in the grand entry, so we've got to hurry," she said, thrusting the dress into Letty's hands so she could help.

Leaving the sling's strap around her neck, Letty slipped her arm out so her fingers would be free to lace up the corset back as fast as possible. Then she hurriedly clasped a white fur cape at Princess Maisy's throat for warmth before they rushed to the stairs.

Prince Cassius waited at the bottom, wandering aimlessly around the grand entry.

"Finally," he grumbled loudly.

"I'm sorry to keep you waiting," Princess Maisy called down the staircase. She lifted her skirt gracefully as she descended the steps.

Letty followed behind, instantly annoyed by Prince Cassius's attitude. It wasn't so hard to be patient, was it? Getting the princess changed had taken seven minutes at the most. Prince Cassius really hadn't wasted any time in confirming what Letty already feared: this was going to be a long morning.

"Just a moment," Prince Cassius said to Princess Maisy as she and Letty reached the bottom of the stairs. "Is *she* coming with us?" He almost sneered the word "she," as though it were a dirty thing, flicking his eyes at Letty as he did.

"Pardon me?" Princess Maisy asked, blinking quickly, shocked that the prince had said such a thing.

Noting that the princess could not seem to form a reply, Letty quickly stepped forward to address the prince herself. "Yes, Princess Maisy asked me to come along," Letty stammered. "I grew up in the village, so I know it quite well. I'm happy to guide you around." She pasted on a smile, trying to make sure that *someone* would be pleasant if the prince wouldn't.

"Yes, that is exactly right," Princess Maisy said, finally snapping out of her stupor. "Letty, who is both my good friend and my lady-in-waiting, has been very gracious to offer her expertise. I think you'll enjoy the tour very much—at least, I should hope so. I may be biased, but I am convinced there is no place in the world quite as beautiful as Trielle." She smiled good-naturedly.

Letty couldn't help but marvel at how perfectly Princess Maisy handled the situation. She had stood up for Letty without directly scolding the prince and then redirected the conversation to a more comfortable topic with a bit of playful teasing. The princess really was quite excellent with people when she wanted to be. *It must be her years of diplomacy lessons taking charge,* Letty decided.

Prince Cassius extended his arm to Princess Maisy, who accepted it gracefully.

"I think one glance at Pelorias would change your mind about that, Your Highness," he said.

Letty fell into step a few feet behind the two of them as they began down the cobblestone road. It didn't take long for lanterns to appear on both sides of the lane. Although they were not lit during the day, the lanterns still added a certain beauty and elegance to the lane as they hung high above the ground, and Letty's heart swelled with appreciation for this lovely place she called home.

Princess Maisy turned over her shoulder to speak to Letty. "Why don't you come up in front of us? That way you can show us the most interesting things and lead the way if there's somewhere you would like to show us."

Letty picked up her pace to pass Princess Maisy and Prince Cassius and take the lead. "Well, this is Lantern Lane," Letty said, addressing her commentary mostly to Prince Cassius, whom she assumed knew much less about the kingdom of Trielle than Princess Maisy.

"Very interesting," Prince Cassius replied. Then, turning to Princess Maisy, he added, "What are all the lanterns for?"

Princess Maisy looked taken aback that the prince had addressed his question to her instead of Letty, although Letty wasn't particularly surprised. Even though the princess had explicitly established

Letty as the expert of this area, Letty hadn't expected that it would earn her the prince's respect.

"Ah. Well," Princess Maisy said, composing herself, "it's a safety measure so that travelers from the mountains—especially from Pelorias—can get to the villages in the dark without accidentally wandering into the forest."

Prince Cassius nodded appreciatively. "Innovative and beautiful," he said. "I'm sure if we had a forest dense enough in Pelorias, we would have done the same thing."

"I'm sure you would," Princess Maisy replied flatly.

The three of them continued down the lane. As they walked, Letty pointed out various buildings and scenery, adding brief comments here and there. Prince Cassius didn't seem to take much interest in them, although Princess Maisy nodded and encouraged Letty along.

"This is my papa's dry goods shop, and my home right above it," Letty said as they passed in front of the tall building with a sign over the porch that read *Lantern Lane Dry Goods*.

"Oh, Letty, how lovely," Princess Maisy gushed. "Is your family inside? If we're here already, we might as well say hello."

What a prospect that was, introducing Miles and Mama to Princess Maisy and the visiting prince! A smile spread across Letty's face. She was about to say, "Oh yes, let's!" but before the words could leave her mouth, Prince Cassius interrupted with a childish groan.

"Let's continue on, or turn back if you'd rather—I don't care which—but let's not stop here."

"Whyever not?" Princess Maisy asked.

"I don't want to stop in an old dry goods shop to meet a few commoners," he complained. "Unless you forgot to mention that they're noble in some way, I don't see why they deserve a royal visitation."

Letty watched as Princess Maisy's teeth clenched. The princess calmly removed her hand from the prince's arm and turned to face him. "It's possible that you aren't aware of how rude and arrogant that comment would sound to me. We're not talking about just anyone; it's Letty's family. And even if they weren't, they would still be people, and people deserve respect." She stole a glance in Letty's direction. "*All* people, royal or not. Even servants and their families."

Prince Cassius shifted, clearly uncomfortable. Any cheerfulness was now replaced by awkward tension. "Of course. I'm sorry, Your Highness. I didn't mean to upset you." He glanced at Letty, just as the princess had, but he didn't offer an apology to her. "Perhaps it's best if we turn back," he said.

"Yes, perhaps it would be best," Princess Maisy said with a defeated sigh. Once again the prince and princess began walking, in the opposite direction this time, and Letty found herself trailing behind again. *Well,* Letty thought, *at least the princess didn't have enough time to get her dress dirty. And I suppose the cook was wrong: I didn't have to spend the whole morning with the prince after all.*

CHAPTER 5

Letty added two sugar cubes to Prince Cassius's tea, just as he had requested the day before, and prepared Princess Maisy's tea exactly as she liked.

"Has she added enough cream for you, Your Highness? And enough sugar? I know you prefer your tea a bit sweet," Prince Cassius asked anxiously.

"Yes, it's just fine," Princess Maisy answered him with a polite smile. "Thank you, Letty."

"Of course. Is there anything else I can do for either of you?"

Prince Cassius shook his head, busy smothering a scone in jam while stealing glances at Princess Maisy.

"No, thank you. I think we're all right," Princess Maisy said. "Oh, but Letty—" Princess Maisy pulled Letty just a bit closer and lowered her voice a touch. "I left a little something for your . . . friends on the vanity chair in my bedroom. See if the kitchen has something to contribute, too."

Letty grinned. "Yes, Your Highness," she said. "Enjoy your tea."

"Have I told you yet how beautiful your dress is?" Letty heard Prince Cassius say as she walked away. Letty couldn't help but giggle. Despite the princess's boldness that morning—or perhaps even because of it—the prince seemed quite smitten with Princess Maisy.

It took a great deal of self-restraint for Letty to walk normally back to the castle from the garden. What she really wanted was to race back as fast as she could and see what Princess Maisy had left her. She knew exactly what the princess meant: she had found supplies for Letty to bring to Papa and Rylan in the dungeon.

Once she was out of their sight, she indulged herself a little and ran the last few yards to the castle's entrance, then continued at a brisk pace to the princess's chambers—definitely *not* running, she convinced herself.

Sitting on the vanity chair, just as Princess Maisy had promised, were two warm blankets and a small stack of books. "Papa is going to love these," Letty whispered to herself as she picked up the books and examined them. There was a Bible, a book of poetry, and two novels, all beautifully bound in leather with gold titles imprinted on the spines. Letty decided to leave the things there while she dashed down to the kitchen as the princess had instructed.

"Oh, there you are, Letty," one of the kitchen hands said as Letty entered the kitchen. "The food Princess Maisy asked for is over there." She tilted her head toward one of the tables, where Letty saw a small basket filled with leftover berries from the day's breakfast, along with a full loaf of bread, some nuts, and cheese. How thoughtful of the princess to have had it prepared ahead of time!

"Thank you!" Letty said as she collected the basket from the table. She was gone as quickly as she came in, hurrying back to the princess's room to grab the books and blankets before rushing outside and around the castle.

She wondered suddenly, as she stood in front of the cellar doors, what she was supposed to tell whichever guard was standing down below. Would he be as understanding as Clement had been? She supposed there was only one way to find out. She squared her shoulders, set down the awkward bundle of blankets, books, and food that she had been cradling in her arm, and, still using only her good arm, managed to lift the heavy door—not much, certainly not enough to get herself in with all of her supplies, but enough to call to the guard down below.

"Hello?" she called down. "Could you please come hold the door for me for a moment?"

Letty heard heavy, thudding footsteps, and then the face of an unfamiliar guard appeared.

"State your business," he said gruffly.

"My name is Letty, and I have supplies to bring down, but only one good arm at the moment." She wiggled her shoulder just a bit to demonstrate what she meant and was pleased to find that the movement was less painful than it would have been a day or two before.

"Supplies for storage?"

"No, sir, supplies for the prisoners."

The guard's eyes widened for a moment, and then his brow furrowed. "I can't let you in here, miss. Where did you get your information, anyway?"

"I'm under Princess Maisy's orders. She was concerned about their living conditions, so she asked me to bring food, blankets, and books to pass the time. That's all I have here. You're welcome to check it all."

"The princess's orders, you say? And why did she choose you to be her messenger?"

"I'm her lady-in-waiting," Letty explained. She hesitated, wondering if she should add the real reason she had been sent. It could backfire, certainly, but in the end, Letty decided that honesty was the best path in this situation. Besides, if the guard only thought she was a random messenger, he probably wouldn't let her stay and talk very long, and she desperately wanted to talk to Papa. "She also sent me because one of the prisoners is my father."

"What proof do you have that the princess sent you? How do I know that you aren't here to conspire with your father?"

Letty considered for a moment, racking her brain for anything she could show or say that would be strong enough evidence to convince this guard that her story was true. Nothing surfaced. She shook her head. "I don't have proof, but I give you my word that I'm telling you the truth. I just want to bring these things that Princess Maisy sent and talk to my papa for a while. That's all."

The guard's eyes narrowed, and he stared intently at Letty for a long moment. Finally, he replied, "All right." He climbed the stairs and held the door up with one strong arm, and with the other, he helped Letty gather the things she had brought. "But if I get the sense that anything is questionable, you'll have to leave immediately. Do you understand?"

"Yes, sir."

Letty passed beneath the guard's arm and waited at the bottom of the steps for him to close the door. She noticed wood shavings scattered around her feet, and a rounded piece of maple wood lying next to a pocketknife. "Is this a hobby?" she asked.

The room dimmed as the guard lowered the door. "It passes the time."

"What are you making?"

The jingling of his keys echoed against the stone walls as he said, "I don't know yet," and inserted the key into the heavy iron lock. Metal ground against metal before there was a click, and the guard pushed the door open.

"You have a visitor," he barked. Then, to Letty, he added, "Remember, no funny business." He dropped the books he had been carrying for her, and they hit the ground with a thud, stirring up a cloud of dust. The door closed heavily behind Letty.

Rylan had been staring at the ceiling as he lay on his worn, narrow cot in the corner of the room, and Papa, who had been pacing from wall to wall before the door opened, now rushed to his daughter.

"What are you doing back here?" he asked as he pulled her into his embrace. "And where did you get all this?"

"Princess Maisy asked me to deliver it to you."

Papa's hands moved to Letty's shoulders, and he stepped back to look at her.

"Princess Maisy? Why would she send you with these things?"

"She wanted to make sure that you were properly taken care of."

Papa put one hand to his temple and closed his eyes as he massaged it, as if hoping that what he had just heard was not true. "Letty, does this mean you told the princess?"

Letty hung her head for a moment and then looked up directly at her papa, meeting his gaze straight on. She had made the choice to bring the princess and Jocelyn in on the secret. With a hard swallow, she nodded.

"What exactly did you tell her? And how were you even *able* to speak to the princess?" Papa paused to take the food and blankets from Letty's arm. "In fact," he grunted, "I have about a hundred questions that I didn't get to ask the last time you were here. Why are you at the castle in the first place? How are Miles and your mother? How did you hurt your shoulder?" He stopped again, drew a deep breath in through his nose, then released it as a sigh. "Sit down and tell me from the beginning."

And so she did. After spreading one of the new blankets over Papa's cot, Papa and Letty sat down next to each other, and Letty began by telling him about how she, Miles, and Mama had gone up the mountain to look for him when he didn't return from his trip. Rylan sat up in his corner to listen to the tale as she described the terrible snowstorm, Miles's fractured ankle, and how scared and disappointed they all had been when they realized that Papa had never made it to the hut on the mountain.

"It sounds like you were very brave," Papa said.

Letty went on to explain how Miles had taken over running the shop, and when Letty was making a delivery, Princess Maisy had seen her on the street and mistook Letty for her lady-in-waiting; how even though Miles's best friend Peter had tried to help her, the princess had still forced Letty to come to the castle; and how rude and cruel the princess had been at first. She described their pivotal argument and their apologies afterward, and she told him about how the guards had found Princess Maisy's *real* lady-in-waiting, Isla, but Princess Maisy had promised to improve her behavior if Letty would stay.

Letty mostly skipped over the night Miles had told her the search parties were giving up—Papa already knew all about that part. But she turned to Rylan as she explained how she had learned that he was missing, too.

"Thank you for caring so much about my family," Rylan said with tears in his eyes. "I'm sure Kiana appreciated that visit very much."

"I'm happy to do what I can," Letty replied. "Elsie and Liam are the cutest little things." She then went on to tell Papa and Rylan about preparing for the prince's arrival and how she had hurt her arm while redecorating the guest rooms. Finally, she told them about Prince Cassius's arrival and how much Princess Maisy's changed demeanor contrasted with his. "And then, when I found you," she concluded, "I couldn't handle all of it on my own. I just *had* to talk to someone. Since you asked me to keep it secret from Mama and Miles, I went to the most trusted people I had besides them."

"How can you be sure they're trustworthy?" Papa asked with deep concern.

"They're my friends, Papa. Jocelyn's been helping me all along the way, and Princess Maisy promised to help me any way she could—the food, blankets, and books should be evidence that she kept her word on that. She also promised not to tell her uncle."

Papa sighed and relaxed a little. "I have always trusted your good judgment. I can see that it wasn't fair of me to expect you to carry that knowledge all on your own. I do hope they can keep quiet and that Mama and Miles don't get pulled into this mess."

"Or anyone on Lantern Lane, for that matter," Rylan cut in. "For everyone's safety, the fact that we're here needs to stay as secret as possible."

Letty's head dropped into her hands, and she wove her fingers into her curls. "But why?" she groaned. "If others knew what happened and why you're here, we could get help! You have a lot of friends who would vouch for you. Maybe Miles would know what to do. Someone can help. Just tell me what happened, Papa!"

Rylan shifted on his cot. "I don't know, Jasper, maybe she—"

"No," Papa interrupted firmly. "Rylan, no. I do not want my daughter involved in this. Look at us. If we tell her why we were arrested, she'll end up right here next to us, and you know it."

Rylan nodded and looked down, and Papa turned back to Letty.

"I'm not going to tell you, Letty." Papa was kind but firm. He looked up at the opening high on the wall. "I'm sure it will be suppertime soon. You should go. The princess is probably waiting. Please thank her for sending you with these useful things. We will be much more comfortable tonight."

"Oh, all right." Letty recognized that tone in Papa's voice well, and she knew it would be no use to argue further. She was crushed by the disappointment of still not having the answers she wanted, but she resolved that this would not be the end of the discussion, and next time she would get the information she sought.

Letty stood and gave Papa one more hug, then waved to Rylan as she made her way to the door. The dungeon door had no handle on this side; Letty supposed it made sense to prevent prisoners from escaping. She knocked hard on the door, and from the other side, the guard cracked the door open slightly.

"It's just me, don't worry," Letty assured him. "The other two are still sitting on their cots."

The guard pushed the door a fraction more, peeking in to make sure Letty was being honest, then swung it wide enough for Letty to step out. "Good timing," he said. "It's almost time to change watch, and I don't know if the next guard will be as easy for you to convince as I was."

"Thank you. I appreciate your help and understanding," Letty said. She really was grateful, but she was certain that her voice didn't sound like it. She was still upset by all the secrecy, perhaps even more now than she had been on her first visit. What was so dangerous about whatever Papa and Rylan had done that *nobody* could help at all? It all seemed ridiculous. Feeling as turbulent as a hurricane, Letty shoved the overhead door open just enough to slip out. With a deep breath, she gathered control of her stormy emotions. She needed to appear as normal as possible to not draw undue attention. After a moment, feeling more collected, she carefully headed back to the castle.

CHAPTER 6

On an ordinary evening, Letty would be helping Princess Maisy into her evening gown. Perhaps she would arrange the princess's hair and send her off to supper before going to eat in the kitchen. This, however, was no ordinary evening. Jocelyn had joined Princess Maisy and Letty in the princess's chambers to help both of them prepare for the ball.

While Jocelyn focused her attention on Princess Maisy, Letty swished her skirt in front of the mirror, hardly able to believe that the image staring back at her was real. She had never worn anything so magnificent in her life. The ball gown she had been given was originally designed for Princess Maisy in preparation for the prince's arrival. In fact, it was one of the gowns that had upset Princess Maisy so much that she had snapped at the seamstress, and then at Letty. After the princess realized how inappropriate her behavior had been and promised to do her best to change, Letty had helped her apologize to the seamstress and her assistant. The princess had decided that most of the dresses they had designed would be suitable with some adjustments, but she had asked for an entirely new ball gown that she thought would suit her better. Now, as Letty stared at herself in the mirror, she was so glad the princess had made that decision. The gown was a gorgeous turquoise color with flowers embroidered all down the front. The hem fell in the perfect place, just brushing the tops of her feet rather than pooling a few inches on the floor as it had when Princess Maisy tried it on. The loose, ruffled sleeves fluttered gently across Letty's shoulders before the neckline formed a gentle V shape. She had even been able to take off her sling for the evening since her shoulder was feeling significantly better. Everything came together beautifully; Letty couldn't have been more thrilled.

"You look absolutely lovely, Letty," Princess Maisy said.

Letty turned around to face Princess Maisy and gasped. "You do, too, Your Highness."

It was true: the princess was stunning in her floor-length gown, with its red, silky underlayer showing through the top layer of nearly sheer black organdy. The sleeves puffed out ever so slightly, and the well-fitting bodice cinched at the waist before flowing into a full, elegant skirt.

Princess Maisy smiled softly. "Thank you."

"Yes, you both are beautiful. Now hurry up—we've got to get your hair done," Jocelyn said, herding Letty and Princess Maisy toward the vanity.

Although Letty was a guest at tonight's ball, she was still a lady-in-waiting, and one who was quite good at styling Princess Maisy's hair at that. So, despite her royal-looking gown, she began twisting and braiding the princess's thick, dark hair into an elegant updo. When she was finished, Princess Maisy gave up her chair, and Jocelyn took over styling. Letty knew that her thick, wild brown curls were difficult to tame, but Jocelyn managed well, pinning most of her curls in a neat pile at the back of her head and leaving a few particularly lovely ringlets hanging by her ears and face.

"You look as though you could be a princess yourself tonight," Princess Maisy said after Jocelyn placed the last pin in Letty's hair.

"I feel like it," Letty replied. "Thank you for the invitation, Your Highness. I can't wait for tonight."

"You're welcome," murmured the princess. The corners of her mouth turned up, but there was a nervous look in her eyes.

Jocelyn slipped out of the room to go help the maids in the kitchen as they prepared to serve the guests who would begin flooding into the castle any moment now. Meanwhile, Princess Maisy wandered over to her bedroom window and stared blankly out of it.

"Is something the matter?" Letty asked.

"No. Yes. I don't know!" The princess plopped down onto the windowsill and leaned her head wearily on the side.

"Well, why don't you talk me through what you're feeling?"

Princess Maisy sighed. "I think Prince Cassius will propose marriage tonight," she explained. "My uncle has been planning to have our betrothal all arranged by the time the prince and his family leave for Pelorias, which will be tomorrow morning. I don't know if it will be at the ball or afterward, but I'm certain that he will propose, and I . . . I don't know what to do. I don't want to say yes."

"Is it still the same issue we discussed the other night?"

"Yes, very much. He treats me just fine, but some of the things he does—like what he said on the walk yesterday—irk me so badly.

It's like . . . it's like when you told me a real prince would care more about kindness and grace and things like that than he would about nice gowns and perfect decorations. A prince should be more concerned about his own character than bragging about how much better his kingdom is than all the others or showing off all the time."

"It's simple, then. If he proposes, just say no."

"You have no idea how angry that would make my uncle."

"Why?"

"Well, because that's the way he planned it, I suppose. I . . . I don't know, really."

"If the king just wants to make sure you marry a prince, there are others you can choose from."

Princess Maisy continued staring out the window and let out a puff of air, causing a little white cloud to form on the glass. "I'll think about it," she muttered. "But I suppose we'll cross that bridge when we get to it. In the meantime, hurry and finish any last touches you need. The ball will be starting soon."

The sounds of chatter floated up the stairs from the grand entry as guests began to filter into the castle. Letty ducked down to take one last look in the vanity mirror, nervously adjusting the curls left out from her updo as she tried to remember the plan. *When the noise starts to die down, I'll slip down the stairs and join the last few people making their way to the ballroom,* she reminded herself. *Then all I have to do is blend in with the crowd and wait for Princess Maisy to make her entrance.*

"Would you help me brush on just a little bit of rouge?" Princess Maisy asked. "I can't make it as light and natural as you do."

"I'll do my best." Letty took the small container from the princess, listening intently to the noise level downstairs as she fulfilled the princess's request.

"Does it sound like people are moving into the ballroom to you?" Princess Maisy asked as Letty swept the small brush across her cheeks.

Letty paused her movement to focus on listening. "I can't tell. There's so much noise; it's hard to know whether it's from the grand entry or the hallway." Just then, the first few faint notes of violin music danced from the ballroom into the princess's chambers.

"Listen to that!" Princess Maisy exclaimed. "People must be moving into the ballroom now. Hurry, you've got to go join them."

Letty swept one final brush on each of Princess Maisy's cheeks. Then, with a smile and a wave to the princess, she darted out of the room and down the hallway. She slowed as she approached the corner. She tilted her head high and pulled her shoulders back. Her goal was to avoid being noticed as she descended the stairs, but if she were, she wanted to make sure she looked like she belonged there. Tonight, she wasn't some fourteen-year-old girl, a villager, or even a lady-in-waiting; she was an honored guest of the crown princess of Trielle.

The crowd was slowly moving to the ballroom. Most of the guests had their backs to Letty as they waited their turn to press through the grand doors, so it was simple for her to glide down the stairs—quite gracefully, she thought—without being noticed by more than one or two people with whom she exchanged a brief smile and nod before joining the waiting throng.

It was thrilling to be a part of a crowd so full of excitement and life, not to mention nobility. Every one of them was dressed as elegantly as Letty had ever seen, with men in black, white, navy, and burgundy tailcoats while the women sported gowns of all kinds and colors, complete with ruffles, flowers, lace, and frills. From inside the ballroom, Letty could hear the bright, cheerful chirps of the flute combined with the soulful tones of the violin and cello, the harp plucking melodically along with them. It was some of the most beautiful music Letty had ever heard. As she drew closer, she could see the small orchestra against one wall, and the chandeliers glistened overhead, casting a golden glow throughout the ballroom.

"What a lovely gown, young lady," said an older woman as she passed by Letty, smiling while gently waving her hand fan in front of her face. Letty returned her smile and watched as the gentleman she was walking with escorted her away.

Letty stood near the wall and watched as all the noblemen and women exchanged polite greetings and made small talk with one another. Letty wondered if she would be able to find someone to talk to.

"Ladies and gentlemen," a loud voice proclaimed from the doorway. A hush fell over the ballroom as everyone stopped talking to listen, and even the musicians paused their piece. "May I present Prince Cassius, crown prince of Pelorias." The crowd dipped into curtsies and bows as Prince Cassius appeared in the doorway, looking as regal and haughty as ever in his white tailcoat with gold buttons and, of course, his jewel-set crown. "And," the announcer added, "Queen Adelaide and King Dorian of Pelorias." Once again, the guests bowed and curtsied in acknowledgement.

King Dorian surveyed the scene before him with his chin held high and his nose turned up.

"And finally, may I present King Henrick of Trielle and his niece, Crown Princess Maisy of Trielle." Far deeper now, the watching throng bowed, then burst out into soft applause as King Henrick escorted Princess Maisy into view.

Prince Cassius approached the princess, took her hand, and bowed. Letty was just close enough to faintly hear him ask, "May I have the first dance, Your Highness?"

Princess Maisy nodded, and as the music started back up, he escorted the princess to the center of the ballroom. Off they went, stepping and twirling across the ballroom floor.

CHAPTER 7

Prince Cassius and Princess Maisy waltzed around the dance floor as the rest of the guests looked on with admiration. Letty pushed her way through the crowd so she could watch the couple.

As the prince and princess twirled through the room, Letty could see one face, then the other, switching every few seconds. She saw Prince Cassius's face first, his gleaming brown eyes fixed on Princess Maisy as he guided her. His mouth moved, but to Letty's disappointment, she couldn't hear his words. She tried to read his lips—something about the princess being beautiful, perhaps—but she couldn't be certain.

Princess Maisy's face appeared next. The corners of her mouth turned up in a sweet smile, but she was not nearly as fixated on the prince as he was on her. She glanced only briefly at his face, then returned to looking over his shoulder at the clusters of guests forming a circle around them. She replied when he spoke to her but seemed perfectly satisfied to watch her guests in between the short bursts of conversation.

On and on it went this way until at last the musicians played their final drawn-out chord, and the song was over. Princess Maisy curtsied as the last notes drifted through the air like the end of a sweet memory that would be too quickly forgotten. Prince Cassius responded with a deep, sweeping bow, and all the guests clapped.

Princess Maisy's eyes met Letty's as the orchestra struck up another song. Several other couples made their way to the dance floor, and Princess Maisy turned to say something to Prince Cassius. He looked past the princess at Letty. He frowned, then nodded reluctantly, and Princess Maisy glided over to Letty.

"Well, what do you think?" Princess Maisy asked. Her sparkling eyes and smile were much brighter talking to her friend than they had been while she danced with the prince.

"It's gorgeous," Letty replied. "The music, the people, the dancing—all gorgeous."

"I thought you might like it."

Letty glanced over Princess Maisy's head at Prince Cassius, who had stepped away from the dance floor, now occupied by a dozen other noblemen and women, and was glaring disapprovingly at Letty.

"Somehow, I get the feeling that the prince doesn't like me very much," Letty half joked.

Princess Maisy shook her head. "I don't think it's so much that he doesn't like you as it is that he simply thinks he's better than most people."

"Except for you."

The princess sighed. "I know. I guess being a princess makes me an exception." She lowered her voice to a soft murmur. "He told me I was beautiful while we were dancing."

"I thought that was what he said." Letty looked over at him again, and this time found Prince Cassius with his arms crossed, tapping his foot impatiently. "I think you'd better get back to your dance partner."

Princess Maisy swiveled to look over her shoulder. "I suppose you're right. Well, enjoy the rest of the ball, Letty. I'll come find you later if I can get a moment."

"Have fun, Your Highness," Letty said as Princess Maisy strolled away. Once the princess was close enough, Prince Cassius immediately struck up a conversation. *Princess Maisy was right,* Letty thought. *He's almost certain to propose.*

At just that moment, a young man—perhaps the same age as Princess Maisy, or at least close to it—approached Letty. He had dark skin with eyes the color of Mama's chocolate cake and curls tighter than Letty's. He also had a beautiful smile and wore a royal blue suit with small silver buttons all the way up the front of his suit coat. He smiled his charming grin at Letty, then extended his hand to her.

"Would you like to dance with me?" he asked.

Letty accepted breathlessly. She hadn't *really* expected to be asked to dance; she hadn't planned to be much more than an excited but casual observer to the events of the evening. Still, she accepted his invitation by returning his smile and placing her hand in his. Letty discreetly rolled her shoulder, testing it for pain. Finding none, her smile widened. The young gentleman guided Letty's left arm to his shoulder. He placed his hand on her back, taking her other hand in his, and began to step in time to the music.

Perhaps it would have been wise for Letty to join Princess Maisy for a few of her dancing lessons. Letty hadn't even considered how she would look if she *did* somehow end up dancing at the ball, but here she was, and she wished she had given it more thought. She stared at her feet, trying to force them to follow the young gentleman's movements.

He chuckled. "I take it you have not danced in a while?"

Letty's cheeks flushed. "You could say that. Actually, I haven't danced much at all before," she admitted.

"Really? Your mother never had you in dancing lessons or anything like that? I thought that was quite common."

Letty only shrugged in response.

"Well," he continued, "you're improving already. Just follow my lead."

For the next several measures of music, he guided Letty through the steps while she tried hard to look at him instead of straight down at her feet. After a moment, he spoke again.

"By the way, I don't believe we were properly introduced. I'm Count Alder. And your name?"

"Letty."

Count Alder waited a moment as though expecting more from her response—perhaps a title or a noble family name. When she didn't add anything else, he continued. "Ah, well, lovely to meet you, Letty. May I ask which part of the kingdom you're from?"

Letty smiled at that. She certainly wouldn't mind talking about home. "Of course. I live very close by, on Lantern Lane—you know, the road that leads up to the castle?"

Count Alder's eyes widened for a brief second, just barely long enough to be noticed. "How lovely," he said, smiling at her again as he recovered from his apparent surprise. "I didn't know there was anyone living there that could be considered nobility—most of the houses seem rather small, you know."

Letty understood his confusion now, and her smile faltered a little as she realized that the count thought she was a noble, just like him.

"Oh, well, I . . ." Letty knew that in all likelihood, she was about to make this conversation very awkward. She didn't get the chance, though, before Count Alder hurried on to correct himself.

"Not that they aren't beautiful, of course, and there's nothing wrong with a smaller home. I just didn't expect . . . well, I'm sure you know what I mean."

Letty laughed softly. "Don't worry; I know what you mean. You're right—they are a bit small, but I'm actually not noble." She said the last three words slowly, as though afraid they might bite her as they left her mouth. "I'm Princess Maisy's lady-in-waiting."

"Ah, a . . . lady-in-waiting? I see."

The last few measures of the song felt much longer than the rest of it had, and each misstep made Letty feel more and more self-conscious. At last, the final note was played, and Letty and Count Alder exchanged a bow and a curtsy.

"It was a pleasure to make your acquaintance," said Count Alder. "I hope you enjoy the rest of the ball." Then he slipped away from Letty and almost instantly was back on the dance floor with a new partner.

Perhaps that's enough dancing for now, Letty decided, strongly influenced by her very limited skills. She moved to the outskirts of the ballroom, happy to observe the couples on the dance floor, and especially watching for any glimpses she could catch of the prince and princess. They danced together almost every song, although once or twice the princess was stolen away by some other partner for a dance. Each time they danced together, it looked very much like the first dance: the enraptured prince, captivated by the princess, who spoke kindly and danced beautifully but did not reciprocate the same kind of interest.

Besides being able to see so much of everything, another benefit of being at the edge of the crowd was that, as she drifted slowly through the magnificent sea of people, Letty could hear many of their conversations. Most of them were not very interesting—ladies chatting about parties they had attended and gowns they had bought, lords and counts and gentlemen of all other noble rankings discussing weather and business—things Letty didn't care much to listen to. In fact, she wasn't *trying* to listen to anyone—that is, until she recognized the low, murmuring voice just behind her.

"Just look at them, how well they get along on the dance floor." It was King Henrick's voice, and Letty realized with a start that King Dorian was on his other side. She froze, hoping they wouldn't notice her presence.

"Yes," King Dorian drawled in reply. "I think it's safe to say that the alliance we discussed is certain." He lowered his voice even more, and Letty found herself straining to catch his words. "And that gold, of course—"

"Shh. Not here," King Henrick hissed.

Warning bells rang in Letty's head. She knew something was very wrong with what she had just heard, but before she had time to think about it, her attention was caught by a wail from the violin.

It wasn't just Letty whose attention had been caught; the whole orchestra stopped playing, and every guest in the room turned toward the now-silent musicians. It seemed, however, that this was the intention, for standing next to the violinist was Prince Cassius, looking quite pleased with the attention that was on him.

"Princess Maisy," he boomed, "would you come join me, please?"

The crowd parted to let the princess through. She walked slowly, and her face turned a bright crimson. Letty shoved her way to the front of the onlookers, directly next to the prince, not caring anymore how ladylike and noble she did or did not seem.

At last, a dazed Princess Maisy made it to the waiting prince. He took both of her hands in his, staring intently at her for a long moment, although the princess quickly turned away from his gaze.

"I thank you all for your attention," he continued in a tone that carried through every corner of the ballroom. "I have a very important announcement to make."

Letty held her breath. *Here it comes, here it comes,* she thought, twisting her dress nervously.

Prince Cassius turned from the crowd to fully face Princess Maisy, though his voice still rang performatively through the room. "Your Highness—Princess Maisy—I have come to adore you. Your boldness, kindness, and grace are captivating, and all are qualities I wish my future queen to possess."

Princess Maisy's eyes were wide and frightened, but Prince Cassius didn't seem to notice. "I have decided that we should become betrothed."

The ballroom burst into wild applause as Princess Maisy stood still as a statue in front of the prince. He gazed at her with adoration. "You will have me, won't you, my darling?"

This question seemed to awaken the princess from her stupor. Her head turned, searching, until at last her desperate eyes locked with Letty's. That single look communicated everything—all that Letty and Princess Maisy had discussed before the prince had arrived, all the effort Princess Maisy had taken to develop the qualities that Prince Cassius admired, and all of her worries that she had told Letty about over the past few days. Letty was positive that Princess Maisy knew what she needed to do, but it was clear that she was afraid. Letty nodded her encouragement, and Princess Maisy took a deep, shaky breath.

"No, Your Highness," Princess Maisy said, her voice so soft that Letty could barely hear it, even as close as she was. "I cannot accept."

CHAPTER 8

Wh-what?" Prince Cassius spluttered. He was no longer trying to project his voice to the entire crowd. "What do you mean? Are you saying you won't marry me?"

"That is what I'm saying," Princess Maisy replied. "I'm sorry, Your Highness. You are a very charismatic man with many talents, but that is not enough for me to marry you."

Prince Cassius gawked. "What more could I have done to win you over?"

"This doesn't seem like the place—"

"I want to know. Just tell me."

Princess Maisy shook her head. "I don't want to criticize you, Your Highness. I'm in no position for that. But I suppose if you want an explanation, I'll simply say that I have been working hard recently to overcome my faults—especially my pride and my tendency to be less kind than I should be. I want to marry someone who will do that work with me, but it doesn't seem to me that you would."

"I don't understand."

"Well, take Letty for example." Princess Maisy gestured in her direction. Letty's instinct was to shy away from the many eyes that were turning to see whom the princess was talking about, but she reminded herself that Princess Maisy needed her support right now, and she stayed put. "It must have been a dozen times in the past three days that I've reminded you of her name or asked you to be polite to her, but all you've shown her is disregard and disdain."

Prince Cassius grasped Princess Maisy's hands tightly. "But why make this about her?" he implored. "People like her, even like all these others, these 'nobles,' they're different from you and me."

Princess Maisy looked the prince straight in the eye and pulled her hands away from his. "I don't think so."

"Princess!" King Henrick bellowed. Everyone in the path of the king darted away from him and his wrath, revealing him to Letty and Princess Maisy. His shoulders were high and tense, his face bright red in a very different way than Princess Maisy's had been when the prince declared his love for her. His jaw was clenched, and he marched toward his niece. "What is the meaning of this?" he hissed.

Princess Maisy gulped but stood her ground. "I mean exactly what I said, Your Majesty."

King Henrick glared at the princess as though he would rip her in half if he could. Then he whipped around to face the crowd. "Everybody out!" he bellowed. "The ball is over. Go home."

The guests all started murmuring among themselves, growing gradually louder by the second. Letty overheard many passing comments about how disappointed guests were to stop dancing, some about how terrible it was to invite people to a party and then send them home early, and others complaining that supper had not been served yet. Still, no matter what complaints they had, the crowd began to disperse, exiting the ballroom the same way they had entered just over an hour earlier.

"Princess, a word," King Henrick growled. He took Princess Maisy by the wrist and pulled her after him, pushing through the throng to reach the enormous ballroom doors. Princess Maisy looked back over her shoulder at Letty with teary eyes that couldn't seem to stop blinking, and the corners of her mouth turned down in a hard, nervous line. Her face showed a feeling that Letty knew all too well—in fact, Letty was starting to feel it herself as her heart rate quickened and her chest pinched a bit tighter. King Henrick was clearly furious, and the princess seemed afraid to suffer the consequences of her decision.

Letty gritted her teeth. *Be brave. Be brave,* she told herself as she began to follow the king and princess out of the ballroom. *If Papa were here instead of in the dungeon, he would do the same thing.*

King Henrick stormed up the stairs with Princess Maisy in tow, and once Letty managed to burst through the dense crowd flooding from the ballroom out to the main castle doors, she followed. The king threw the library doors open, seemingly unaware of the still-departing guests, who, though they could not see the library, could hear the force he used. Letty managed to catch the door inches before it closed, and she slipped inside unnoticed.

"Do you understand the magnitude of what you've just done?" King Henrick raged. Princess Maisy cowered in front of him. She was facing Letty but was, understandably, far too focused on her uncle to see her lady-in-waiting. "You humiliated the crown prince of Pelorias—and thus the entire Pelorian royal family, and I would even go so far as to say all of Pelorias. And what's more, you did it in public, in front of every person of any noble ranking in the whole kingdom!"

"It's not my fault that he proposed at the ball instead of waiting to do it privately," Princess Maisy defended herself shakily. "I couldn't very well accept his proposal and then turn around and decline once everyone left."

"There was no need to decline!" King Henrick shouted. "You were *supposed* to accept. That was the plan, remember? What did we go to all the trouble and all these preparations for if you were just going to turn him down, you selfish girl?"

"She didn't *know* she was going to turn him down, Your Majesty," Letty spoke up from behind him. King Henrick whipped around, glowering at her but too stunned to speak. Letty took the opportunity to say her piece, although her legs were screaming at her to run, and her heart seemed to think it was racing against a wild colt. "The princess has legitimate concerns about Prince Cassius. Do you really expect her to marry someone who would make her miserable? Is it so selfish that she doesn't want to be betrothed to someone she doesn't get along with well?"

Now that Letty had said all she needed to say, she held her breath and waited for the king to react.

"Yes," King Henrick hissed after a long silence. The red in his face began spreading slowly up to his ears, and his shoulders hunched, making him look even larger and scarier than he already was. "Yes, I do expect my niece to fulfill her duties. She had a responsibility to agree to this betrothal, not to listen to the foolish, romantic antics of a child or a servant! You impertinent girl!"

"Your Majesty, please," Princess Maisy implored, "don't be angry with Letty. I made my own choice. Letty only reminded me that I'm brave enough to trust myself with big decisions."

King Henrick swiveled back toward the princess, unsure whether to focus his anger on his niece or Letty. "You are in no position to advocate for someone else right now. Keep quiet."

Back at Letty now, he continued, "I've half a mind to dismiss you right here. For now, at least, you will get out of this library. You will go help the rest of the servants clean up the mess that has been left from this ball, and you will not indoctrinate my niece with any more of your nonsense."

King Henrick shoved past her and stormed toward the library door. Just before he exited, however, he stopped. "And Maisy, you will go to your room, and you will stay there for the rest of the night. Perhaps tomorrow, too." With that, he threw open the library door and swept out.

An empty silence filled his place in the library, settling over Letty and the princess like a constricting force.

"Letty," Princess Maisy whimpered at last, "what did I do?"

"I . . . I don't know. I thought it was the right thing to do—I mean, I *still* think it was the right thing to do. But your uncle . . . I'm sorry, Your Highness. I shouldn't have intervened."

The princess blotted her teary eyes, trying—though not always succeeding—to catch the droplets before they escaped down her cheeks. "No, I'm glad you did. I just don't know what to do now."

"Well, I guess you could start by going to your room." Letty couldn't help but smile a little as she cracked her sad joke.

Princess Maisy sniffled as she laughed. "Yes, I suppose so."

"I should probably go help clean up before King Henrick really does dismiss me," Letty added. She turned to leave but was stopped by Princess Maisy's voice.

"Wait, Letty," she said. "I can't believe you spoke up in front of my uncle like that. You didn't have to. I just wanted to let you know that I appreciate it."

Letty smiled over her shoulder. "You're welcome. Thank you for returning the favor."

Back in her room, Letty carefully draped the exquisite turquoise gown over the end of her bed, sighing at its loveliness and at her regret over the disastrous evening. Once she was back in her lady-in-waiting clothes, she replaced her arm sling. Her shoulder felt pretty good through the evening, but the doctor had told her to wear the sling for about a week, and she still felt nervous that she might hurt it again as she went about her duties. Satisfied that everything was secure, she went to check on the progress of the cleanup.

In the grand entry, Letty saw that most of the guests had cleared out, and nearly all signs of the ball had already disappeared. In the kitchen, the cook shooed her away and said they had plenty of help. With no work to do, Letty decided to slip outside for a breath of fresh air.

The guards at the doors knew her now, so she had no trouble exiting, and she moved to the darkness of some trees as she watched the final few carriages make their way down Lantern Lane, their elegant designs faintly illuminated by the lanterns' glow. She sat in the cold grass and let her fingers dance through its dying blades. Staring up at the stars, Letty breathed deeply as she tried to encourage the stress to leave her body.

Before she could fully decompress, however, the front doors flew open once again. Letty froze when she heard the two deep voices and two sets of angry, thundering footsteps leaving the castle.

"Please, King Dorian, let me fix this," King Henrick implored. "The princess was just frightened in front of the crowd. She will agree to the betrothal once she's had a few minutes to calm her nerves, I'm sure of it."

"It's too late," King Dorian's voice fumed. He was carrying a small trunk, and Letty assumed he intended to load it into his carriage. "She humiliated my son in front of half your kingdom, not to mention that you wasted days of our time on this pointless visit."

"But the alliance we discussed—"

"It's over! That agreement was dependent upon this betrothal, and that's been canceled."

"But King Dorian, you can't just turn away from the gold!"

"I never cared about the gold. Our agreement was that there would be a union of the crown when my son married your niece, and in return, you would get the help you need. It looks like neither of us will be getting what we wanted." He turned away from King Henrick, ending the conversation, and continued his march toward the carriage house.

King Henrick remained planted in place, kicking at the ground and muttering furiously to himself. Most of what he said was too quiet, but Letty clearly heard the words, "Everything, ruined!" She held her breath in the darkness, praying desperately that King Henrick wouldn't stray far from his spot or peer too intently into the night. If he did, he would be furious that she wasn't doing as she had been told, and adding that to the anger Letty was already witnessing couldn't end well for her. Thankfully, the king kept his back to Letty most of the time, and when he didn't, he seemed too distracted to notice the shadow of a girl sitting a few yards away from him on the castle lawn.

After several agonizing minutes, King Dorian at last came stomping back to the castle.

"Call for your footmen and have them carry the rest of our trunks down to my carriage," he said, ordering King Henrick around like a servant rather than the ruler of a kingdom. "My family and I will not waste another night here."

King Henrick continued trying to convince King Dorian to stay as he followed the fuming man back into the castle. "Please, Your Majesty, just listen . . ." His words were cut off as the door closed behind them.

Letty heaved a giant breath of relief. Now all she had to do was make it back inside and find something to clean before she had another opportunity to get caught disobeying the king. The guards opened one of the doors, and Letty scurried inside, quiet as a mouse. She instantly set to work with the first group she laid eyes on—those sweeping and mopping the dirt and any lingering shoe prints from the floors in the grand entry.

Mopping and sweeping weren't exactly Letty's favorite things to do, but such monotonous, thoughtless work gave her plenty of time to reflect on what she had just heard. What was this about an alliance, and, even more confusing, why were they talking about gold? King Henrick was obviously furious about it, whatever it was.

Perhaps, she thought, trying to determine how she could get more information to fit all these puzzle pieces together, *it's time to pay another visit to the dungeon.*

CHAPTER 9

Letty didn't tell the princess of her plan the next morning; Princess Maisy didn't need anything else to worry about. After Prince Cassius, King Dorian, and Queen Adelaide had officially left the castle the night before, King Henrick had once again berated Princess Maisy for refusing the prince's proposal. Letty was quite certain that the princess had cried herself to sleep, and she was quieter than usual when Letty helped her get ready for the new day.

"It will be strange to go back to your usual schedule now that we don't have to worry about special preparations anymore," Letty said, hoping to prompt a conversation.

"Yes, I suppose it will be," Princess Maisy replied distractedly.

It was clear that no useful conversation would be happening this morning. Perhaps Princess Maisy just needed some personal space to process all that had happened during the prince's visit, specifically during the ball. That was all right with Letty, though. While the princess was absorbed in her thoughts, Letty had absolute freedom to think about what she needed to tell her father when she visited later and perhaps even come up with a few questions he might be willing to answer. She visualized a list being written, including items such as the strange meetings between King Henrick and the tall, cloaked messenger; the anger the king had expressed after

Princess Maisy turned down the prince; and whatever it was Letty
had heard about alliances and gold.

When at last she finished the princess's morning routine,
making slight changes to accommodate her arm sling, Letty
escorted Princess Maisy down to breakfast, then hurried to the
kitchen. She wanted to get in and out as fast as possible so she
could maximize her visiting time.

The tables and counters were still piled high with untouched
food from the night before. Letty was sure that the cooks and
kitchen hands were less than pleased to see so much food—not to
mention the weeks they had spent preparing it—go to waste.

"Excuse me," she said to one of the kitchen hands who was
passing by. "What is the king planning to do with the leftover food
from the ball?"

The kitchen hand shrugged her shoulders. "The king would have
us throw it away, but I think we'll send some of the staff out this
afternoon to give it away to villagers instead. If you'd like anything,
though, feel free to take it."

That was exactly what Letty had hoped to hear. Casually, trying
not to draw much attention to herself, Letty began slipping apples
and bread into the deep pockets of her gown. She loaded up her free
hand with a stack of sweet and savory pastries, then left the kitchen
quickly. She felt a bit guilty that she wasn't waiting for Jocelyn as she
normally did, but she was certain Jocelyn would understand.

The guards at the castle doors hardly noticed Letty as she left.
After all, why would they pay attention to her? Her presence was
such a usual part of life at the castle now that they didn't give it a
second thought.

How strange, Letty mused as she exited the castle and made her way around the corner to the cellar-style doors. *I've been here long enough that it's normal for everyone to see me. Even I'm beginning to feel like I belong here.*

Any other time, Letty probably would have pondered this for a while longer. Right now, however, she had to focus on the cellar door before her. She hadn't considered how difficult the door was to open when she filled her hand with pastries, and she suddenly regretted her decision. She couldn't set these down as easily as she had the basket she had brought on her last visit. After looking around for a solution, Letty began balancing the pastries in the sling on her other arm. When she finally emptied her hand, Letty slowly and shakily pulled the door open, careful not to let the pastries tumble to the ground.

"You need some help out there?" a gruff voice called from below. Letty breathed a sigh of relief. It was Clement, the guard who had first allowed her to come visit her father. He knew, at least vaguely, of the situation, which meant she wouldn't have to explain everything all over again to another guard.

"Yes, please!" Letty replied.

In an instant, Clement's face appeared below the door. "You again?"

"I really need to talk to my father. Plus, I have food for him."

"I can't keep doing this for you," Clement said with a shake of his head, but he simultaneously helped her with the door. "How long do you need?"

Letty hesitated. "About an hour? I should probably leave when breakfast ends."

Clement shook his head again. "That's a longer time than I'd like . . . but I don't switch positions for another few hours, so I guess it should be all right."

Letty thanked him as he opened the door, and she stepped into the dungeon once again.

The cell was the same as usual: the same dull stone walls and floor and the same meager cots along the walls, although Letty was pleased to see that the blankets and books she had brought last time seemed to be getting used consistently. The only other differ-ence was that her papa was still lying on his cot, his blanket moving up and down in a slow, steady rhythm. Rylan was sitting upright on his cot, reading from the stack of books in the corner, but he looked up when Letty entered the room.

"Letty!" he whispered. "It's good to see you. Your father is still sleeping—I think he had trouble falling asleep last night."

"Oh, no," Letty said. "I really hoped to be able to talk to him. I don't want to wake him up, though, if he's really tired." The sagging of her pockets reminded her that, if nothing else, she should deliver the food she had brought for the two men. "Well, here, at least take this." She emptied her pockets of their contents and removed the pastries from her sling. As it turned out, a sling was not the best place to keep pastries, which Letty discovered when several of them were much crumblier than they had been when they were placed there, and she could feel the resulting crumbs uncomfortably nestled in her elbow. Still, the joy on Rylan's face when he saw the treasure trove of food made the crumbs well worth it. He immedi-ately began feasting, carefully separating about half of the food into a pile for Papa.

"If you don't mind my asking, what were you hoping to talk to him about?" Rylan asked in between bites. "Anything I could help with?"

Letty sat on the floor next to him; both had their backs to Papa. She kept her voice low so she wouldn't wake her father. "I don't know. There have just been some strange things going on, and I wanted to see what he thought about them."

Rylan cocked his head to one side. "Strange things like what?"

Letty took a deep breath, trying to picture the list of topics she had imagined earlier that morning. "Well, for example, there were two different times that I saw King Henrick out in the gardens, talking with some strange cloaked messenger."

Rylan's eyes opened wide. "Tell me more about that."

Letty closed her eyes, trying to remember exactly what had happened the first time she'd seen it from the guest bedroom window. "Well, I was cleaning the guest bedrooms, and I happened to look out the window and saw a tall, thin man in a cloak climbing the garden wall. I was worried at first, and I was going to report it to the guards, but then King Henrick stepped away from the shadow of the wall and talked to him. Their conversation seemed pretty animated, and then the messenger left."

"Interesting," Rylan said thoughtfully. "You said it happened twice, didn't you? Was the second time the same?"

"Yes, except the second time, I opened the window just a little. I didn't hear much; I caught just a few words. Something about the princess and . . . gold, I think." The wheels in Letty's head began spinning. "Just like King Henrick talked about with King Dorian the other night. The messenger must have been from Pelorias."

"That makes sense. What other strange things have happened?"

"Well, King Henrick has seemed very stressed about Prince Cassius's visit. Then, last night, when Princess Maisy rejected the prince's proposal—"

"The princess rejected a proposal from the prince of Pelorias?"

"Yes. They weren't a good fit," Letty explained. "Anyway, after she said no, King Henrick was furious. I heard him begging King Dorian to stay and telling him that the princess would change her mind. Then, like I said earlier, King Dorian said that their alliance was off, and he was talking about how King Henrick wouldn't have his help with gold."

Rylan's eyes stayed wide, and his lips pressed together as though he were fighting to keep them shut.

"Is there something you can tell me about that?" Letty asked.

Rylan looked over his shoulder. Papa was still asleep on his cot, snoring lightly. Rylan beckoned Letty to come in closer and quieted his voice so much it was hardly even a whisper. "At the end of Lantern Lane, there is a mapmaker," he began to explain.

"Oh, yes, I think I heard something about maps from the window, too." Then, suddenly remembering, she added, "And I found a map in the library that Princess Maisy said was wrong—I don't remember how, though."

Rylan nodded. "A few months ago, that mapmaker—his name is Abel—was hired by King Henrick to create some new maps of Trielle. The king told Abel that the borders on these maps would look a little bit different; he said it was part of some kind of agreement that was being sent to the king and queen of Alria."

"That's right," Letty said, the image of the map now recreating itself in her mind. "Princess Maisy said that the borders of Trielle were on the wrong side of the Alrian mountains on that map."

"Exactly," Rylan confirmed. "The agreement was supposed to be some kind of deal to purchase that part of the Alrian mountains. At least, that's what King Henrick told Abel.

"What Abel didn't know is that King Henrick had no intention of making a deal with Alria. He was going to try to trick them out of the land."

"But why? How?"

"Because there's gold in those mountains, Letty, and King Henrick wants it. He hired Abel to make these new maps, and then he sent spies to Alria to secretly replace the maps in the Alrian palace with these new ones."

Letty's mouth gaped open. "The king really thought he could take the gold just by switching a few maps? How ridiculous!"

"It sounds that way, doesn't it? But think about it: if Alria doesn't have any true maps, they don't *really* have any proof that they own those mountains or the gold in them, do they?"

"I guess not . . ."

"And if the king of Pelorias agrees to take some of those maps as well and go along with it . . ."

"Oh, I see. So that's where the visit from the Pelorian royals comes in, right? The plan was to make an alliance where King Henrick has their support for his lie, and King Dorian gets unity of the crown for Trielle and Pelorias so that his son can rule both kingdoms one day. Am I understanding that right?"

"Yes, that's right. But King Henrick didn't expect that one of his men would turn on him."

Letty's eyebrows shot up. "Really?"

"Yes. King Henrick apparently didn't tell his spies the purpose of their mission when he sent them out, but one of them—the mapmaker's son, Torin—figured out the king's plan, and he foiled it. He swapped the maps back and destroyed his father's new maps that had been sent."

"How did you find out about all this?"

Rylan looked over his shoulder again at Papa, who still seemed to be sleeping peacefully. "Well, Torin is a good friend of mine, and when he returned, he told me about it and asked for my advice. Then he told his father, Abel. Abel was so upset with his part in it that he decided to turn to the wisest man he knew for advice—"

"Papa," Letty whispered. "And King Henrick found out."

Rylan nodded somberly. "Yes. When another messenger went to confirm that the mission had been completed, the king learned what Torin had done. He ordered Abel to make more maps, but Abel refused, and the king threw both of them in a prison far away, on the other side of Trielle. Somehow along the way, the king found out that your father and I knew about it, too. I guess he was scared that we would tell people how corrupt he was, so he had us imprisoned here—only until he can find somewhere else to send us, I suspect."

Suddenly, a stern voice came from behind them.

"Rylan," Papa said. "Stop speaking now."

CHAPTER 10

"Papa, I—" Letty began, but Papa was staring intently at Rylan and didn't let her finish.

"How much did you tell her?" he demanded.

Rylan hung his head, refusing to meet Papa's eyes. "I told her everything. I'm sorry. But she was already starting to put things together for herself, and I figured she deserved to know."

"We've talked about this countless times, Rylan. It isn't safe for Letty to know." His voice grew sharper with every word. His harshness surprised Letty, considering how calm and gentle his demeanor typically was.

"Papa, Rylan is right. King Henrick is corrupt! But now that I know, I can stop him, and then you'll both be freed—"

Papa crossed the room suddenly, surprising Letty with his strength and speed after being confined so long in the dungeon. He grabbed Letty by the shoulders and didn't speak until their green eyes had locked with each other. When he finally did start, he was slow, clear, and as loud as he could be without catching the attention of the guard outside. "You will not speak to the king," he insisted. "In fact, you will avoid the king at all costs. You will not spread this information around the servants or the villages, because that will only put a target on your back like it did for us. Keep quiet, don't get in trouble, and promise me you won't do anything foolish, all right?"

That was a tough list of demands for Letty. She was itching to storm right up to King Henrick and announce to him that she knew all of his secrets, but she understood why that wouldn't be the best idea. After all, if the king could have Papa and Rylan arrested without anyone knowing, how difficult could it be for him to make a fourteen-year-old lady-in-waiting disappear? And she wasn't one to gossip to strangers, only to discuss concerns with people she trusted, so she felt like she could agree to that as well. But not doing anything foolish? Well, Letty wasn't entirely sure she knew what her father meant by that, but anything that Papa considered foolish she would probably find frightening anyway—just the kind of thing Letty preferred to avoid. After taking a moment to consider all this, Letty nodded. "Yes, Papa, I promise."

Papa nodded. His face softened a bit, as though comforted by his daughter's reassurance. "Remember, Letty, if King Henrick finds out what you know, you will be in danger, too. Don't let him find out."

"I know."

"Then you should leave now. The more time you spend lurking around here, the more likely it is that you will get caught at some point. I don't think it's wise that you keep coming to visit."

Letty wasn't so sure about that. After all, she had visited three times now, and she had never had any problems. But she nodded anyway so that Papa wouldn't worry and gave him a hug before she left.

"Don't forget to eat. I got crumbs all over my elbow to bring you those pastries, so you had better enjoy them," Letty joked on her way to the door. As always, she knocked a few times on the door to let Clement know she was finished, and he pushed it open to let her leave.

"Good conversation today?" he asked as he turned the key in the lock to secure the prisoners once again.

Letty could feel the tips of her ears beginning to turn red, and her heart skipped a beat. Had Clement heard their conversation? And what would he do if he had? Letty did her best to suppress the redness that threatened to creep across her cheeks and forced a smile onto her face. "Yes, it was very nice, thank you." She caught her breath, waiting to see if Clement would say something else.

Clement only gave a small smile and said, "That's good. I'm glad to hear it."

Letty exhaled deeply as Clement led her to the steps that would take her back above ground. Maybe, just maybe, he hadn't heard anything after all.

She thanked Clement again once she arrived at the top of the steps. She poked her head up through the door, looking around like a frightened groundhog to make sure all was clear before she emerged. Something felt different leaving the dungeon with all the information she had now. Like Papa had said, the world suddenly seemed more dangerous, so she was extra cautious as she walked back to the castle.

One of the guards at the castle door looked familiar to Letty: it was the guard who had been in the dungeon a few days before when she had gone down. She flashed a quick, close-lipped smile as she approached.

He cocked one eyebrow. "Down there again, eh?"

Letty's head snapped up, and her eyes were wide as she looked at him. She glanced at the other guard to see if he had heard the comment as well. It seemed that he had but was not particularly worried about it. Letty turned her full attention back to the first guard and said very slowly, "I had an important delivery to make."

He shrugged. "I was just asking."

Letty scurried the rest of the way into the castle, suddenly feeling paranoid. The guard had been so casual when he'd said it, and even though he wasn't specific, it wouldn't take long for anyone to realize what he had been talking about. Should she go back and ask him to keep quiet or not to mention that she had been in the dungeon at all? It seemed like a good idea. Then again, it was possible that if she asked him to keep it secret, he would get suspicious and concerned enough to go to King Henrick and report her. She shook her head once, deciding against it. It was better to hope he didn't care enough to mention it to anyone else than to go advertising that the king wouldn't approve of her visits.

Still, even though she didn't think he would bother telling the other servants, every glance had Letty fearful. Each look from another maid or footman sent Letty into a wave of worry, wondering if they knew where she had been. Head hanging low, Letty rushed to the library, where the princess would be arriving any moment for her lessons.

Letty felt like her lungs would not fully expand as her breathing turned ragged. This was all so much to wrap her head around. She needed to talk to someone immediately. Princess Maisy would be here soon, and Letty could see what she thought—but no, the princess had to spend far too much time with King Henrick to be safe with that information. What if she accidentally said something that gave it all away? She could always run to find Jocelyn . . . but the more she thought about it, the more *anyone* in the palace felt too close to the situation for comfort. There was really only one solution, although Papa would be upset if he knew: she would go home tonight, and she would tell her family. Just Miles, at first—he would help her decide how much detail was okay for Mama to know.

Certainly, Miles will know what to do, she thought.

CHAPTER 11

Letty fidgeted through Princess Maisy's lessons all morning, and she couldn't have repeated a word the tutor said if her life depended on it. All she could think about was maps, gold, spies, and the borders between kingdoms. She could see now why Papa had been so opposed to her having any part of it: safety concerns aside, it was all just so muddled and confusing. She was anxious to get home and have Miles's help to sort it out.

Letty wasn't sure what Jocelyn talked about during the luncheon, either. After skirting Jocelyn's question about where she had been that morning, Letty's ears all but tuned out the sounds around her as Jocelyn chattered through the meal. She felt guilty for not listening better, but she couldn't help how preoccupied her mind was. It wasn't until she was helping the princess prepare for supper that she finally broached the subject of going home for the evening.

"Your Highness," Letty began as she fastened the princess's gown—a navy blue silk tonight, "there are a few things I need to talk to my family about tonight. Is it all right if I go home once we're finished here? I may spend the night there, too, if it's fine with you."

"Of course. Is everything okay?"

Letty knew she shouldn't lie, but she needed advice, and she didn't feel ready to talk about the king to Princess Maisy. She bit the inside of her cheek and mumbled, "Everything is fine. I just want to go pay them a visit, that's all."

Princess Maisy looked at her narrowly. "Are you sure? You have seemed stressed and absent all day."

Letty nodded. "Yes, Your Highness. I just need to see my family. It's been a long week."

Princess Maisy shrugged. "That's all right with me. There's nothing exciting happening here anymore, anyway." She scoffed. "Did you know that my uncle had the servants bring him his meals in his quarters instead of in the dining hall, just so that he wouldn't have to see me?"

The corners of Letty's lips turned down, her mouth flattening like a wilted rose petal. "I'm sorry, Your Highness," she said at last. "I didn't know this would cause such a big rift—"

Princess Maisy waved her hand dismissively. "No, no. I'd rather eat alone every day than have to make small talk with Uncle Henrick. It is always an unpleasant conversation. Anyway, you're welcome to go home tonight if you'd like."

Letty thanked the princess and hurried to finish getting her ready, which didn't take long this evening, since Princess Maisy wasn't particularly concerned with the way she looked. "I don't know why I'm bothering to change into an evening gown, to be perfectly honest," the princess chuckled. "I guess dressing up to go eat by myself is a little silly."

Letty hesitated. If she didn't get to talk to Miles soon, she thought she might explode. Then again, the princess sounded lonely, and Letty didn't want to just leave her here by herself. She drew a breath and slowly asked, "Would you like me to stay and have supper with you?"

Princess Maisy's eyebrows lifted quickly, and a grin spread across her face. "Oh, no, that's not what I meant. You go spend time with your family. Thank you for offering, though."

"Are you sure?"

"Yes, Letty, I'm sure. I'm sorry. I didn't mean to make you feel guilty; I just needed to complain for a minute."

"Well, in that case," Letty said, brushing a bit of dust from the princess's shoulder, "I think you're ready for a nice, peaceful supper."

"That's a good way to think about it." Princess Maisy laughed.

Letty escorted Princess Maisy downstairs to the dining hall. She paused outside the door. "Are you positive I can go home right now? I'll wait until after supper if you'd like."

"Absolutely positive. Have fun tonight."

Letty nodded, although she wasn't sure that "fun" was a word she would use to describe her plans for the evening. While she wandered back to her room for her shawl, Letty pondered exactly how she was supposed to tell Miles that Papa hadn't actually died, as he thought. It wasn't the kind of thing one could casually drop in the middle of a conversation. Did something need to preface such a revelation, or was it better to get straight to it? It didn't help that the story only got wilder as it went on. She wasn't sure how Miles would react to the news of the king's corruption.

All the way home, Letty practiced having the conversation in her head. *Hello, Miles, it's so good to see you. I found Papa. He's in the dungeon.* That didn't sound quite right. *Do you remember when you came to the castle to tell me that Papa probably died? Well he didn't. In fact, he was only a few feet away at the time.* She shook her head. That didn't come across the right way, either. She didn't want to stun Miles, just share the information with him so they could have a conversation about it. The closer she got to home, though, the more she realized that she would probably have to accept that he would be shocked—really, there was no way around it.

The bells above the front door of the shop jingled as Letty pushed it open. Miles, who was behind the cash register counting the day's earnings, beamed when his eyes landed on her. He grabbed the single crutch beside him and jammed it under his arm, then dragged his fractured ankle behind him as he went around the counter to meet his little sister.

"Your ankle is getting better, I hope," Letty said.

Miles pulled her into a brotherly embrace, tousling her hair a bit in the process. "Yes, it is. And you did something to your arm. What happened?"

Letty blushed. She'd forgotten that her brother hadn't seen her with her sling yet. "I first hurt it by falling while I was trying to hang drapes, and then I tried to help hang a heavy painting and—well, you see."

Miles winced. "Maybe next time you can try waiting until you've recovered from an injury before you go and make it worse," he teased.

The corners of Letty's mouth turned up in a faint smile, but she was already distracted as she tried to listen for footsteps above them. "Is Mama home?" she asked when she didn't hear any movement.

"Not right now, no. She'll be back soon, though; she's just delivering a loaf of bread." Miles leaned across the counter to finish his counting and lock the register for the night. "Actually, it's a bit of an interesting errand." He spoke slowly, as though he had to grab and force each word into line before it could leave his mouth. It sounded very much like the way she had been imagining she would tell him of her father's imprisonment, and the tone made her ears perk up. "We recently found out that Papa was not the first man to go missing on Lantern Lane. In fact, a few weeks earlier—at least, we think—two men went missing at the same time, a father and son."

Letty's breath caught in the back of her throat. Thank goodness Miles already knew this piece of the puzzle! It would make explanations much easier, she was sure of it. She was ready and excited to launch in right then and there with all the information she had acquired about these men, but Miles kept talking, completely oblivious.

"Of course, people didn't notice as quickly because it's only the two of them living there and because the father is a bit of a recluse, I guess. Apparently, though, their neighbors started getting worried because they hadn't seen them in a few weeks, and when they went to go check on them, their neighbors realized they were gone. Mama went to see if any of their close neighbors have any more information about what might have happened. I think there's a connection between them."

"Yes," Letty was finally able to interject. "Papa was friends with the mapmaker, right?"

Miles nodded enthusiastically. "Yes, he came to the shop

sometimes and . . ." Miles trailed off. "I didn't say it was the mapmaker. How did you know?"

"Let me get you the register stool first," Letty said. She stepped around to the other side of the counter and hefted the tall, sturdy stool. "I think it might be best if you sit down for this conversation."

Before she could get Miles seated and ready, though, the bell above the door jingled again, and in walked Mama, looking exhausted and dejected, an empty basket on one arm. With her other arm, she slowly rubbed the back of her neck, her face pointed at the floor.

"Nothing, Miles," she muttered. "Nobody had any clue—" Just then, Mama looked up and saw Letty standing next to Miles, the stool still clutched in her hands. "Letty! Oh, my days, I didn't expect you home. I am so glad to see you." She dropped her basket on the counter and pulled Letty into her arms as best she could, considering that Letty was at least a head taller. When she seemed satisfied with the embrace, she pulled away, and her eyes shifted back and forth between Letty, Miles, and the stool, which Letty had hastily set down to hug her mother. "What are you two up to?"

"Letty was just about to tell me someth—" A quick, sharp shake of the head from Letty quieted him instantly.

Later, Letty mouthed dramatically. Miles gave a subtle tip of his head, then looked back to Mama, whose attention was fixed on him, waiting for his answer.

"What I mean to say is, we were just talking while I finished closing up," he corrected himself.

Mama looked around the shop. "Well, it looks like you're just about finished. I don't have anything fancy ready, but what do you say we all go upstairs and find something to eat?"

Mama turned to the stairs and led Letty and Miles up to the kitchen. While her back was turned, Miles looked at Letty quizzically.

Papa? he mouthed.

Letty nodded, and Miles's eyes went wide. Letty forced herself to turn away and follow Mama. It would be so hard to wait until Mama was asleep to talk to Miles, but she reminded herself that she needed to talk with Miles first and make sure it would be okay for Mama to know. Mama was the last person anyone in the family wanted in danger. She stared at Mama's back as she made her way up the stairs and prayed that Mama would be tired enough to go to bed early tonight.

CHAPTER 12

"Psst, Miles, are you still awake?" Letty whispered from the doorway of his bedroom. The whole house was dark; Mama had gone to bed about half an hour before, and Letty had been waiting patiently until she was quite sure Mama was really asleep.

"Yes. I was worried you had fallen asleep," Miles whispered back. The darkness was broken by a small, flickering orange flame as Miles lit a match and touched it to the wick of a tall candle. "What were you going to tell me earlier?"

Letty looked over to Mama's room, where she could just barely hear the soft sound of her mother's breathing.

"Can we go downstairs to the shop so our talking won't wake Mama?"

Miles's eyes flicked back and forth between his fractured ankle and his crutch. "I think I'll be louder going down those stairs than I would be talking, but if you insist." He shrugged.

"Just keep the noise down as best you can," Letty begged. "I can try to help if you need me to."

Letty carried the candle so that Miles could focus on getting his crutch to land softly with every step. She kept close behind him, wincing with every audible step or dragging sound from his foot. As they approached the stairs, Miles stumbled, and Letty's hand flew to her mouth to cover her gasp. Thankfully, he managed to catch himself—although with a thump too loud for Letty's comfort—and he quickly steadied himself. Letty held her breath and listened for any noise indicating that Mama had heard, but all was still.

"You know, it might be easier to walk if the light was in front of me instead of behind me," Miles suggested.

"Oh, right. Sorry." Letty hurried to take the lead, casting the candle's faint glow down the stairs instead of at Miles's back. Slowly, carefully, quietly, they made their way down to the shop, testing each step for creakiness before placing their weight on it. At last, both Letty and Miles made it to the ground floor. Letty fetched the stool for Miles, then sat on a crate facing him.

"As long as we're still quiet, I think we should be able to talk here," Letty said.

Miles nodded. "Then hurry up and start talking. You know something, and I've been waiting all night to find out what it is."

"Well, you already know about the mapmaker and his son. That's a piece of it," Letty explained. She forced a fast breath out of her lungs. "I don't know the best way to explain this story. It's complicated."

"Just start from the beginning," Miles urged her. "Or, at least, the closest you can get to it."

Letty thought for a moment. What *was* the beginning of this story? "I don't know if I'll get all the details exactly right, but here it is as best as I know it. The mapmaker—his name is Abel—is one of the best in the kingdom. A while ago, maybe a month or two, King Henrick hired him to make several copies of a new map, one that showed Trielle's borders just a little differently."

Miles's brow furrowed. "Different how?"

"Bigger. Going over a part of the Alrian mountains, to be exact. Apparently, King Henrick has thought for a time that there might be gold there, and his men found it. So he hired Abel to draw up some new maps showing that the portion of those mountains with gold belonged to Trielle instead of Alria."

"What is that supposed to do?" Miles scoffed. "Just because he has a map that says so doesn't make it true."

"I know, but if all of Alria's maps say the same thing, and so do Pelorias's, then who can say it isn't true?"

"But Alria's maps *wouldn't* say the same thing."

Letty leaned forward, her elbows digging into her knees as she tried to explain. "Exactly, which is why King Henrick sent some of his men to Alria to secretly replace their maps. That way they wouldn't have any proof."

Miles crossed his arms and considered for a moment. "All right, I guess that makes sense. So what happened to the mapmaker, then?"

"His son was one of the men King Henrick sent. The king apparently didn't tell them the whole plan, but Abel's son figured it out and destroyed the maps. Then he came back and told Abel, but he also told Rylan the cobbler. Abel also needed to talk to someone, so he came to Papa."

Miles's eyes widened. "Interesting," he whispered. "Go on."

"Well, when King Henrick found out, he had Abel and his son arrested and sent to some prison far away—I don't know where, exactly. And somewhere along the way, he discovered that Papa and Rylan knew, too." Letty's eyes glistened with excited tears as she continued. "I found them, Miles."

Letty expected Miles's jaw to drop open or that he would perhaps shout in surprise. Instead, he sat still as a statue, staring off into space. He hardly seemed to be breathing.

Letty shifted uncomfortably on her crate, waiting for an actual reaction to the news. After a moment, she noticed a tear rolling down one cheek and realized that Miles's eyes were completely brimming. Another tear fell, and then another.

"When?" he managed to croak out at last.

"About three days ago," Letty whispered, "the day the prince arrived."

"And you didn't tell me?" The hurt in Miles's voice twisted like a knife in Letty's heart. "I thought he died, Letty. Mama is upstairs asleep *still* thinking he's dead. How could you not tell us?"

"I couldn't. I wanted to, really, it was the very first thought I had, but Papa told me not to. Besides, the royal family from Pelorias was visiting at the time—actually, the king of Pelorias is a part of King Henrick's plan, too, or at least he was. Anyway, I was busy."

"Too busy to let me know my father is alive?"

"Miles!"

Miles's head dropped into his hands, and he rubbed aggressively at his face. "I'm sorry," he said, his face still buried. "I'm sorry. Papa told you not to. That must have been difficult for you."

"Papa still doesn't want you to know," Letty admitted. "I just . . . I just didn't know what to do anymore. Finding Papa was one thing, but learning that King Henrick is corrupt and imprisoning innocent men was another. What do you think I should do?"

Miles clasped his hands together, resting his forearms on his knees as he leaned forward. "Where is Papa?"

"In the dungeon of the castle with Rylan."

"What about the mapmaker and his son? Where are they?"

Letty searched her memory, trying to recall if Rylan had mentioned anything specific about their location. "I'm not sure. Somewhere far away."

"But for now, we know that Papa and Rylan are safe?"

Letty nodded.

Miles sat in thought for a moment, then sighed. "Well, I don't know what you're supposed to do, but I know what I'm doing," he said resolutely. "I'm going to find the mapmaker and his son and free them."

Letty blinked rapidly, then a few times extra hard, as though the movement of her eyelids would somehow help Miles's words make sense. "You're going to find them?" she spluttered at last. "Miles, that's ridiculous."

"What's so ridiculous about it?"

Letty scoffed. "Well for one, you still have a fractured ankle and can't walk without crutches. And it was an adventure like this that earned you that fracture to begin with."

"The doctor says I'll be healed up and able to walk again in a week or two," Miles replied. "I'll go then."

"The winter weather will be getting worse soon," Letty added. "Before long, nearly every day will be a snowstorm like the one a few weeks ago. We could hardly climb the mountain in that weather. What if you have to go up the mountain again?"

Miles shrugged. "I'll figure it out."

Letty's jaw began to tighten, and her shoulders tensed; she was getting more frustrated by the second. Why couldn't Miles under-

stand that he was being foolish? "You don't even know where they
are," she protested.

"Letty, there can't be that many prisons in Trielle. Besides the
castle dungeon, there might be a few towers here and there, but not
much more than that. I can find them."

This was exasperating. "But why? It's not your job to rescue
them. Don't prioritize them over Papa!"

Miles looked at Letty somewhat sideways, as though puzzled.
"Just because they don't expect us to help them doesn't mean we're
not responsible to do what we can to help—especially since no one
else has enough information to. We know for sure that Papa is safe;
the others we can't be sure about." He sat up straighter and began
gesturing, illustrating his point with his hands as he spoke.
"Besides, breaking Papa and Rylan out of that dungeon will be
almost impossible. But if we can free the mapmaker and his son
and confront the king somehow, maybe we can make him set Papa
free."

Letty considered that thought. Miles made a good point; it was
almost certain that the best way—perhaps the only way—to get
Papa and Rylan released from the dungeon was to expose the king's
corruption and force his hand. Still, the whole idea made Letty feel
queasy.

"Why don't you wait until your ankle is *actually* better before
you decide what to do? Is that fair?" Letty asked.

"Fair enough," Miles replied, "although I'm quite sure what I'm
going to decide."

That was good enough for now, Letty supposed. She knew Miles
well enough to know he wouldn't back down yet.

"Just one more thing," Letty said. "What do we tell Mama?"

"I don't know," Miles answered after a short pause. "What do you think?"

"I think she deserves to know he's alive," Letty said with conviction. "I just don't know how to tell her without bringing up all the rest, and I'm not ready to tell her all of it yet."

"Me neither," Miles agreed. "Maybe for now we tell her that King Henrick is corrupt, that Papa is in the dungeon, and that she needs to keep it quiet so the king doesn't find out that we all know?"

"That sounds perfect. We'll tell her in the morning."

With that agreement between them, Letty silently put the stool and crate back in their proper places. Then she and Miles crept up the stairs.

"Good night, Letty," Miles whispered as he got into bed.

"Good night," Letty whispered back. Miles blew out his candle, as though putting a final period at the end of their conversation.

CHAPTER 13

Y ou two are awfully quiet this morning," Mama observed as she set a steaming bowl of oatmeal in front of each of her children. "I know it's early, but you're usually plenty talkative, even before sunrise."

Letty and Miles looked across the table at each other. Mama was right; they hadn't been talking much, but that was because they only had one thing to talk about, and it was a difficult topic to bring up.

Letty lifted one eyebrow and tilted her head forward, saying without words, *You tell her.*

Miles pressed his lips into a hard line, and he shook his head slightly. He exaggerated Letty's head tilt, urging her to be the one to speak. *You found him,* Miles mouthed.

"All right, what's all this about?" Mama asked. "Don't think I don't notice all that secretive nodding and whatnot."

Miles stared fixedly at Letty. His message was clearly received: it was Letty who had discovered this secret, and it was Letty who was going to share it.

"Well," Letty sighed, "why don't you come sit down with us, Mama?"

Mama glanced back and forth between her two children. "All

right," she said slowly, pulling out a seat for herself.

"Mama, I have something to tell you, and you might have some mixed feelings about it. You'll probably have some questions, but I probably won't be able to answer them all."

"Letty, you're making me nervous," Mama scolded. "Did you get in trouble? What's the matter?"

Letty took a deep breath. Miles nodded, urging her on. "I found Papa."

It took only a second for Mama to process the words. Once she did, she instantly burst into tears. "He's alive?" she sobbed.

"Yes, Mama, he's alive. Kiana's husband, Rylan, is with him." Letty choked up as she spoke; it was impossible not to get emotional watching Mama's tears flow.

"How? Where?"

"In the dungeon at the castle."

Mama recoiled in shock. "How in the world did that happen?"

Letty chose her next words carefully. "I think that King Henrick is corrupt, and Papa had information that could have exposed him. Rylan, too."

"And if he finds out we know anything about this, we could all be arrested, too," Miles added gently. "So for now, this needs to stay within our family. We have to keep it very quiet."

Mama bobbed her head. Her tears had slowed, and she began to wipe them from her eyes. "Obviously, King Henrick can't know that Letty found Papa," Mama agreed. "But couldn't we talk to people on Lantern Lane and let them know what happened? If there's enough of us, we could all confront the king."

"He'll find out before we get the chance, I'm sure," Miles said.

"They found out about Papa and Rylan. I have no idea how, but they did. I imagine it wouldn't take much for us to raise suspicions."

Mama thought about it, then opened her mouth as though to protest. She apparently decided against it, though, because all she actually said was, "You're right." The three of them paused for a moment. It was sobering to know exactly where Papa was but have no way to get him back. As much as they might hope and wish, there was nothing they could do that would free Papa, and if they tried, they knew it would likely end with their own arrests.

"How did you do it, Letty?" Mama asked after they had sat in that disappointment for a moment. "How did you find them?"

Letty glanced over at Miles with questioning eyes. Was this story okay to tell Mama?

Miles nodded. Letty supposed that learning how it happened wouldn't hurt much now that Mama knew they had been found, as long as Letty was careful not to go far enough to explain why. So she described to Mama all that had led up to it—the winter rose bush that she visited every day and the strange window at the bottom of the wall that she hadn't thought much about. She explained that when Miles told her the search parties were giving up and declaring Papa dead, she found herself crying next to that bush and pleading out loud for Papa; then she thought she heard his voice, but when she tried to call out to him, he didn't answer. She told Mama that she thought, at first, that Papa's voice had only been in her imagination, even though it had felt so very real, but then she heard King Henrick and King Dorian of Pelorias talking about a young cobbler they had just arrested—Letty almost added "for treason," but caught herself just in time. Then she explained how she had talked with Clement, the guard, and gotten him to agree to let her go down to the dungeon to see if that cobbler was Rylan and how surprised she was to find not only Rylan there but also Papa.

"That sounds like quite the adventure, Letty," Mama said, sitting in shock as Letty concluded her story. "Papa must have been so excited to see you."

Letty shifted in her seat. "He was quite nervous, actually. He said it wasn't safe for me to know he was there."

"Ah, I see. I'm surprised he allowed you to tell us about it if he was so concerned."

Letty's eyes dropped to the floor, and she shifted again. "Well, he didn't, exactly. In fact, he told me I couldn't tell you, but I just . . . I needed you to know. I couldn't deal with it all on my own."

"Oh, Letty," Mama said, patting her hand comfortingly. "I wouldn't typically tell you to go against Papa's wishes, but I'm glad you told me." Mama squeezed her fingers around Letty's hand. "It's probably about time for you to get back to the castle, so eat up quickly, and we'll get you on the road."

Letty gratefully complied and ate some spoonfuls of her breakfast.

"One more thing, Letty, before I forget," Mama said. "You should tell Papa that Miles and I know about this."

Letty choked on the bite of oatmeal she had just put in her mouth. "Why?"

"He deserves to know his family's situation, especially if he was worried about us knowing. You should explain to him why you thought we needed to know."

"Mama is right," Miles agreed. "It seems only fair to tell Papa."

Letty sighed. "All right. I'll go down to the dungeon today and tell him," she relented. She finished her breakfast, eating more slowly than she had before to draw out the time. The idea of telling Papa that she had told Mama and Miles any part of his story, much less that she had told Miles *everything*, made her slightly queasy. She was worried that he would be disappointed in her.

At last, Letty was finished eating, and she knew that if she didn't get back to the castle soon, she would be late helping Princess Maisy get ready for the day.

"Would you like me to walk you back?" Miles asked.

Letty glanced down at his ankle. Although it was healing nicely, he was still slower than usual, and Letty knew she needed to hurry to make it back on time. "No, thanks," Letty said. "Keep practicing walking on that leg, though, and maybe you can join me next time," she said with a smile.

Letty snatched her shawl off a chair and hastily hugged Mama and Miles goodbye, then ran out the door and up Lantern Lane toward the castle. She felt much lighter than she had on her way home the day before, like a weight had been lifted off her shoulders. Still, something didn't feel quite right; her shoulders felt lighter, but there was a tightness in her chest, a sense of anxiety that said something was coming.

CHAPTER 14

A chilly breeze swept through Lantern Lane as Letty walked swiftly to the castle, and with it came a cold dampness that sent shivers up her spine. Menacing gray clouds gathered in the distance, threatening to cover more than just the mountain's tips in a layer of white, and Letty pulled her shawl tightly over her shoulders. The castle walls drew nearer, and she was struck by the irony of how they had been built to keep threats out, but no one in the city would expect to need protection from those living within.

Even though Letty felt better after telling Miles everything, she wasn't looking forward to telling her father she had disobeyed him. She hoped he understood that his children loved him. She could still picture his kind face when she made a mistake and he reminded her, "Do the right thing, even when it's not convenient—especially when it is not convenient." Neither Letty nor Miles could just stand by when innocent men were kept in prison, and she couldn't bear the thought of Papa and Rylan living in the chilly, dank castle dungeon. For now, though, all they could do was wait for Miles's ankle to heal—and Letty would be sure to bring the prisoners some fresh blankets.

The wind whistled through the street, casting up flurries of leaves that spun around Letty's feet. She watched them trail up

Lantern Lane toward the castle, and she hurried along after them, looking forward to the castle's warmth. She waved at the guards as she approached, and they nodded stiffly, not making eye contact. As she passed by, another wave of anxiety swept over her, and the hair raised on the back of her neck. Something definitely felt wrong. After a slight hesitation, she continued down the path, her lips forming a silent prayer.

Walking across the large yard, her eyes caught a glint of a reflection in the trees leading to the garden, and when she squinted, she saw Clement standing in the dim light. His eyes were wide as he looked around the yard and waved frantically for her to follow him. Letty checked for onlookers, then ducked into the trees.

Pressing a finger to his lips, Clement led her to a dark section near the wall, surrounded by bushes. Then he turned and whispered, "You can't go see your father anymore."

"What? Why? I was planning to check on him later."

Vigorously shaking his head, he said, "No, you can't. It's not safe for you anymore. Last night, as the guards were eating dinner, Lewis, the other guard who allowed you into the dungeon, told everyone about you. He didn't know it, but the newly appointed captain of the guard was standing nearby and overheard. He was furious. Lewis was relieved of his duties, and we were all ordered to let the captain know as soon as you try entering again."

Fear tightened around Letty's heart as she listened and realized the trouble she had caused for herself, her father, and the kind guards. Guilt rippled through her, knowing she had cost Lewis his job. She had only wanted to take care of her father, not cause problems. "Does Lewis have another job he can fall back on?

Where did he go?"

Clement shrugged. "I don't think he does. He started here as a stable boy soon after his parents passed away. Serving in this kingdom is really all he knows. I don't know where he's going to go."

"I feel terrible." Letty's shoulders slumped. "Why didn't you get dismissed? You let me in, too."

"I didn't tell anyone about it. I also didn't reveal that one of the prisoners is your father, and I won't. I'm positive it would get you arrested."

The world grew blurry and began to spin, and Letty leaned on a nearby tree. Clement looked concerned but did not touch her. "Are you okay?"

Letty shook her head. "I don't know. Who's the new captain? I don't think I've seen him yet."

"He used to be a warden over one of the distant prisons and has a reputation for being harsh. After the Pelorias royalty left, the king seemed determined to increase the castle's surveillance. The new captain has been inspecting security along the castle walls and occasionally checks on the guards. I'm certain Lewis didn't realize he was behind him."

Thoughts spiraled in her mind. Her father and Rylan were living in a cold, damp dungeon with little food or water. The mapmaker and his son were imprisoned in an unknown location. A guard had lost his job and might need help. And now Letty had the captain of the guard to worry about. She didn't know how she would be able to keep up with all these problems.

"Clement, would you be willing to take some blankets and food to my father and Rylan on your next shift?"

Shuffling his feet and shrugging his shoulders nervously, Clement looked around them. "I don't know, Letty. I can't lose this job. I need the money to take care of my parents."

"Please, Clement. I need my father, and Rylan has three young children and a wife at home. I know you're a good man. You have done so much to help me already, and I'm grateful. Please, take care of my father, too. Nobody else can do it now."

The muscles along Clement's jaw tightened, and Letty heard his teeth grinding together. "I'll be guarding the night shift from now on. So I think I can bring them supplies without raising suspicion, but you have to promise that you will not go down there anymore."

"I promise. Can you do one more thing for me?"

Clement sighed deeply. "Depends on what it is."

Letty stood on her tippy-toes, one hand cupped around her mouth as she whispered in his ear.

Clement looked relieved. "Well, that's easy enough. I'll ask around."

"Thank you."

Nodding his head, he leaned forward and whispered, "Please be careful. The castle isn't what it used to be, and the captain is watching you closely now. Don't give him any more reason to suspect you."

"Thank you so much for everything, Clement. I'm so sorry."

The sun peeked over the mountaintops, and the protection of the shadows began to disappear. Clement backed away toward the castle walls, lifting his hands in a shrug. "It can't be helped," he said as he turned.

Letty thought, *But maybe it can.*

CHAPTER 15

Seven gentle chimes rang through the halls, signaling the hour, and Letty fought the urge to run as she passed various servants and guards in the hallways. When Letty turned a corner, she saw two young ladies chatting outside a room, fresh sheets stacked high in each pair of arms. They appeared to be having a lively debate about whether the kitchen's blackberry or strawberry tarts were tastier, and when they spotted her, she began lifting her hand to say hello. Before her arm even left her side, though, they scurried away, avoiding eye contact. The guards posted at the stairs watched her intensely, their heads turning as she passed. Even in the empty hallways, Letty felt eyes on the back of her head, and one time, when she turned around, she could have sworn she saw something tall and white wisp around the corner. Whatever it was, it was gone as quickly as it came. Was everyone watching her, or was it her imagination?

Her footsteps echoed as she walked the last stretch to Princess Maisy's room and frantically twisted the doorknob, slipping into the room and nearly slamming the door behind her. Her head rested against the door as she closed her eyes and took a few deep breaths. When she opened them again, she found a startled Princess Maisy sitting up in bed, staring at her. "Are you okay, Letty?"

Walking across the room to open the curtains, Letty said, "I'm not sure, Your Highness. It's been quite a day."

Princess Maisy tilted her head. "It is only seven o'clock in the morning."

"I know," replied Letty, and with that, she collapsed to the floor, the anxiety and tension releasing in a torrent of tears.

"Letty! What is going on? Should I call for Jocelyn?"

"Oh, I'll be okay in a moment, I'm sure." Pulling her legs to her chest, Letty sat huddled in a ball, carefully avoiding her sling.

Princess Maisy scrambled from her bed and grasped Letty's uninjured arm. "Let's move you to a chair, and I will ask a guard to call her."

At the mention of a guard, Letty groaned, but she allowed the princess to guide her to a chair. "I only need a moment. I'll be fine."

"I insist," Princess Maisy said as she grabbed her robe and started walking to the door. "We will have breakfast here this morning. It will be nice to share a meal with someone. I don't want to sit in the dining room alone again."

Opening the door, she waved a guard over and asked him to have Jocelyn bring breakfast to her room this morning. The man nodded his head, then made eye contact with Letty over Princess Maisy's shoulder. His eyes narrowed as he stood in place for a few seconds too long, causing the princess to clear her throat. "I am hungry."

"Yes, Your Highness." He bowed and left swiftly.

"Well, that was strange," Princess Maisy remarked as she finished tying a knot in her robe and walked back to where Letty was sitting. "This may be an interesting day. Are you going to tell me what's going on?"

Letty took a deep breath. "Do you know the new captain of the guard?"

"Captain Foust? He's not a very nice man. He's very stern, from what I have seen, but he wears a feathered hat that is quite funny. He seems very intent on proving himself to be useful. He's been spending hours with my uncle in his study."

"Well, I don't think he likes me very much."

"What do you mean? I don't think he even knows you exist," the princess scoffed. "For the time being, you can help me get dressed. Since I will not be going to breakfast, we can do something a little more casual. What do you think, a green one?"

Letty stood up mechanically and grabbed a green dress, but the princess slipped behind her and touched her hand gently. "Letty, that is an evening gown. You really are out of sorts."

"Oh. I'm sorry, Your Highness. How about this one? It's cold today." Fetching a wool-lined dress of forest green, she lifted it to take a better look. It had intricately woven winter-rose lace trailing up the neckline into a beautiful, button-up turtleneck. The style would complement the princess's petite neck perfectly while also keeping her warm.

"I have not worn that dress for a while! It's perfect."

The usual morning routine was soothing to Letty and helped her forget her nerves for a time. Just as they finished, a knock signaled Jocelyn at the door.

A head of strawberry-blonde hair peeked through and smiled. "Tired of eating alone, Your Highness?"

"Yes, but that's not why I called you up. Letty has something to tell us."

Jocelyn nodded as she placed the tray on the writing desk. "I may already know a little bit."

Letty gasped. "Does everyone know?"

"About Lewis and your dungeon visits? Yes."

Overcome with frustration, Princess Maisy tossed her hands in the air. "Can someone tell me what is going on?"

Pointing at the tray, Letty asked her, "Why don't you eat while we talk?"

"I hardly have an appetite now," the princess said as she pushed the food away and moved to sit on the edge of her bed. "What's wrong?"

Letty stood and began pacing back and forth, twisting her dress in her hands. She didn't know how she was going to word this, but she hoped the princess would understand that her intentions were good. "You know how I have been visiting my father in the dungeon?"

"Yes."

"Apparently Lewis was telling the other guards about how he let me into the dungeon. The captain overheard and was furious. Lewis was relieved of his duties, and I feel terrible about it, and now the captain suspects me," said Letty, the words tumbling out. She stopped fussing with her clothes and looked at the princess. "You said he wears a feathered hat?"

Princess Maisy nodded in acknowledgment, and Letty began pacing again.

"I think that may be what I saw on my way up to your room. I only caught a glimpse, but there was something long and white that disappeared around the corner before I got a good look at it. So, I'm unsure."

"That sounds like him, and he certainly has authority to be in the castle halls. I don't understand why it matters if you visit your father and the cobbler in the dungeon. Many people have visited prisoners in the past."

Letty bit her lip. She realized there was no way around telling Princess Maisy about the king's schemes. Slowly, she turned and faced the princess, took a deep breath, and said, "Your uncle is a thief." Her declaration was met with wide-eyed shock, but as Letty explained King Henrick's plan to steal the gold found in the Alrian Mountains by switching out old maps, Princess Maisy's jaw dropped. Once she learned that four men were in prison because the plan had been thwarted, Princess Maisy's hand moved to her chest as she sat in utter shock.

"Are you all right?" Letty asked in concern. "Do you need a cool cloth for your head?"

Princess Maisy gave a shaky smile. "I suppose I'm the one who is out of sorts now. This news is so sudden . . . and so terrible." Shaking her head as if to clear her uncle's horrific actions from her mind, she asked, "All this for gold?"

Letty nodded.

"He has more wealth than he could possibly spend in a lifetime!" Then, as if hit by something unseen, she rocked back and gripped the bed beneath her. "You are saying that it is because of my uncle that your father and the cobbler have been thrown in prison?"

"And the mapmaker and his son, though we don't know where they are."

Princess Maisy's cheeks turned a fiery shade of red, and her eyebrows narrowed into a scowl as she stood and began to pace the room. "You're positive my uncle did all this?"

"According to my father and Rylan, yes. My brother found proof of it as well. We also found that strange map in your library, remember?"

Turning sharply to look at Letty, Princess Maisy spoke slowly, each word articulated to perfection. "I can't believe he would do this!"

Letty looked at Jocelyn. Jocelyn looked at Letty. Both girls looked at the princess. Neither of them knew how to react to the cold fury rolling off the princess. On the outside she looked as composed as a perfect princess, but the girls knew her well enough to see her rage beneath the surface. Timidly, Letty said, "I am worried I won't be able to stay here much longer, Your Highness."

"Oh yes, you will!" Princess Maisy argued back.

"How am I going to stay here? Your uncle is the king, and he is obviously okay with throwing innocent people into dungeons at will."

With deep, audible breaths, the princess closed her eyes and said, "Well, then, we need to fix it."

Jocelyn moved to the breakfast tray and asked, "Your Highness, would you like some water or tea to calm you down?"

"No! I want to protect the kingdom before my uncle ruins it."

Letty grabbed a fan off of the desk and attempted to distract her friend with its cool breeze. "My brother thinks if he frees the mapmaker and his son, they can prove the king is corrupt and free my father. Miles intends to search until he finds them . . . and I think I'm going to go with him."

The princess's back straightened abruptly. Slowly, she turned to Letty. "That's the solution. I will go, too."

The two servants looked at one another, and hesitantly, Letty said, "I'm not sure that's a good idea, Your Highness."

Jocelyn jumped in. "I have to agree with Letty. It will be hard to get you out of the castle."

Letty nodded. "It is going to be hard enough to get me out of the castle right now, and don't you think the king will send guards to chase after the princess?"

Snatching the fan from Letty and tossing it on the bed behind her, Princess Maisy looked both girls in the eyes before speaking. "I feel that it's my duty as the princess to fix this wrong and release these innocent men. In a few years, I will be the queen of Trielle, and this is not something I want happening in my kingdom."

Letty was startled to see a change come over the princess's posture and expression. Her shoulders were back and her chin was high, and Letty had never seen her look so regal.

There was a determined look in the princess's eye as she added, "I have also studied maps of the kingdom since I was four years old. I know the roads and landmarks better than even my guards. I can narrow down which prison the mapmaker and his son are most likely to be in. You and your brother need me, even with all the complications."

Letty realized that right before her eyes, the princess, for perhaps the first time, had felt the weight of the kingdom on her shoulders, and she was accepting the responsibility that would soon be hers. Letty smiled admiringly as Jocelyn said, "She actually might be right, Letty."

Letty was quiet for a moment. Despite the potential problems, the princess might be the best way to get her father released. She bit her lip and looked at Princess Maisy, who had probably never spent a night away from the castle. "It may be scary," she warned.

Princess Maisy stood even taller and said, "I will have you and your brother with me."

"It may be cold."

"We will build a fire."

"You could get in trouble with the king."

Princess Maisy shrank a bit at this suggestion. Then she shook her head. "At this point, I don't think he deserves the title of king."

The girls stared at each other gravely for several moments.

Finally, Letty shrugged and said, "Okay."

"Okay?" the princess asked in surprise.

"Okay. As long as we can both convince Miles that we should come along."

With a satisfied grin, Princess Maisy turned on her heel. "Now let's make a plan! Is your brother's ankle still healing?"

"Yes."

"How much longer do you think it will take?"

Letty shrugged. "The doctor said maybe another week?"

"That should be enough time to plan and prepare. For now, we will start working on supplies. We can hide them in my armoire. Jocelyn, will you help with that?"

"Of course, Your Highness."

"Letty, we will study the maps after lessons whenever we can sneak away. I can narrow down which prison I think the mapmaker and his son may have been sent to."

Letty thought of the prison at the castle and asked, "What about Lewis? Is there anything we can do for him?"

Shaking her head, Princess Maisy crossed the room to her breakfast tray. "Sadly, there's nothing I can do for him right now, but when everything is over, I will attempt to get his position back. We need to keep up a perfect image over the next few days. If Captain Foust is following you, we cannot appear to do anything out of the ordinary. We'll have to stick to the schedule: lessons, lunch, garden tea, dinner—nothing will seem amiss. Jocelyn will gather most of the supplies for us so you aren't spotted walking through the halls with mounds of food or blankets."

"We'll need to tell my brother that you and I are joining him," Letty pointed out.

"Write a letter. Jocelyn can have it delivered. Right?"

"Of course! Anything you need, I will help with," Jocelyn replied eagerly.

"Perfect! For now, let's eat breakfast. Letty will write a letter, and we will proceed as if everything is normal." She plucked a strawberry danish from the breakfast platter and bit it determinedly.

The princess's confidence was inspiring, and Letty found some of her tightened nerves releasing. She grabbed a breakfast tart, a pen, and a sheet of paper and began to write.

CHAPTER 16

The next few days went exactly as Princess Maisy intended. The girls heard back from Miles, who said he thought his ankle would be strong enough to leave within the week. He wasn't happy about bringing them on such a difficult and dangerous journey, but even he admitted that Princess Maisy's knowledge of the kingdom could be essential to their success.

With renewed purpose, they fell into a strict routine to avoid suspicion. Each day began at seven o'clock and proceeded as any other. Although their routine looked boring from the outside, their minds churned over whispered plans and analyzed potential problems. The servants and guards relaxed again around Letty as the castle returned to normal, but the captain of the guard still lurked around. Letty spotted his tall, slender frame from afar, and he even got close enough for her to see the thick black mustache nested on his upper lip. It was so fuzzy it reminded her of the caterpillars she loved catching with Elsie and Liam, but the thing that made him instantly recognizable was the ridiculous feathered hat he wore. Even the princess had spotted him on more than a few occasions, but soon the sightings lessened, and they decided it was time to study the maps, which—if they were caught—could land Letty in the dungeon. Despite the danger involved, it needed to happen now.

It was planned to be a light day for Princess Maisy's studies, leaving a large amount of open time. Letty moved through the hallways and quickly found her seat in the library, where Princess Maisy and her math tutor were about to get started. Letty knew listening to numbers and equations would not keep her mind off the dangers ahead, so she was pleasantly surprised when the tutor waved for her to join them. Her gratitude ended when he handed Princess Maisy a small lap harp and Letty a small wooden tube with many holes, saying, "Your Highness, I thought we would approach your lesson in a more informal manner today. I adore listening to you play your instruments, and I am sure your lady-in-waiting will enjoy joining us in some musical play. What are your thoughts?"

Princess Maisy looked delighted. "Oh! This sounds wonderful. Doesn't it, Letty?"

Letty looked at the others, their eyes lit with excitement. She then looked at the strange instrument she had never seen before. "I am so sorry, but I don't play . . . at all."

The tutor smiled. "Ah. Don't worry. This is a recorder. It is for beginner musicians, and I believe you do know some mathematics, do you not?"

"Not nearly as much as Princess Maisy, but I know enough to get by in my parents' shop."

"Well, all you need is the basics for this lesson. Did you know that the study of music involves quite a bit of math?"

The tutor showed Letty five different notes and demonstrated different rhythms of notes: quarter notes, half notes, and whole notes. He explained, "Princess Maisy will be playing a more difficult melody, but you will be playing an accompaniment to hers, with few note changes. A baseline, if you will."

He said this while gesturing to Princess Maisy for support, and she nodded her head in response. "Oh, it'll be easy, Letty. Don't worry. It's just for fun."

It took some time for Letty to understand, but the tutor focused on her, flailing his arms through the air in what Letty learned was conducting. He helped Letty find the beat, and she played from a selection of three simple notes when he indicated. In time, she needed less direction, and while she played her three notes, she listened to Princess Maisy's harp. It was clear to Letty, even with her limited experience, that the princess was a very gifted musician, and at one point, Letty even found herself enjoying the process as her three notes molded into beautiful harmony with the princess's flying fingers. Letty understood how counts of twos, threes, and fours could meet together throughout a song, and it occurred to her that she might actually love to learn an instrument if given the time to practice.

The girls had been playing for a while when movement behind Princess Maisy's shoulder caught Letty's eye. The door to the library slowly opened without a sound, and a long feather stretched through the opening. Letty quickly looked down at the page of music in front of her and did her best to avoid looking at the door. Out of the corner of her eye, she watched the captain of the guard slip into the room and move to the corner.

Letty tried to stay focused on the music, but her scalp prickled, telling her someone was watching her. *Maybe he's checking on Princess Maisy.* But Letty knew. These were the watching eyes

Clement had promised her a few days ago, and even from a distance, they were bright blue, sharp, and piercing, taking in every detail before them. Letty squirmed in her seat. She didn't want the captain to know she was aware of his presence, and in her attempt to be discreet, she missed a few notes, which earned her a frown from the tutor.

"I do believe we have worn our pupil out, Your Highness. Maybe it is time to move on. Thank you so much for joining us, Miss Letty. I hope you enjoyed yourself some."

Letty placed the recorder in his outstretched hand and moved back to her seat. For as long as he remained there, Letty ignored Captain Foust in the corner. Minutes felt like hours, but in time, the feather fluttered away, and Letty spent the rest of the lesson twisting her dress until Princess Maisy stood and said, "Thank you for your time. I would ask that we cut it short for now. I can only take so much mathematics, and I would like to do some private study since it has been a light day otherwise."

"Ah. Of course, Your Highness. The world awaits you in this room," the tutor said as he gestured to the well-stocked bookshelves before cleaning up his supplies. Letty moved to help him while Princess Maisy nonchalantly browsed the book titles.

"Thank you, miss. If you can find a recorder, you might be a decent musician. You simply need to work on your focus." He nodded at her and left the room. Letty followed him to the door, peeking into the hallway as she shut it. The captain was gone.

A deep sigh of relief escaped her lips. She crossed the room to Princess Maisy, who had grabbed several maps as soon as the tutor left and was working quickly to place them. The rolls of parchment lay strewn across a large table, their edges barely touching one another, and while Letty looked at the landscape in awe, the princess reached behind her and grabbed another parchment from the shelf, laying it out in front of them. Letty realized the many maps were turning into a sort of puzzle. Each ended where another began, and the massive kingdom of Trielle lay on the table in all of its splendor. The magnitude of the mountains was shocking; they stretched across three of the five different maps. It took a moment for Letty to find Trielle's castle and her small village, which seemed much smaller in comparison to the countryside.

Letty murmured, "It's breathtaking to see all of Trielle at once like this."

Princess Maisy smiled as she started placing small books on each side of the scrolls to secure them. "It is a big and beautiful kingdom, and we have no reason to steal from our neighbors. Could you help me with the edges so I can study the maps better?" Letty took over the book placing and watched as Princess Maisy analyzed her kingdom. "This larger prison is the newest. Here are all the surrounding Trielle prisons." Her delicate finger darted to a point from one place on the map to the next. "This one is most commonly used for small crimes and is within a day's ride from the castle, but seeing how my uncle doesn't want information of his plot getting out, I have a feeling he sent prisoners to one of the more remote locations along the Alrian Mountains." Princess Maisy used her finger to circle three towers on the outskirts of the kingdom. "It seems like a lot, but each of these towers is old and was built for different reasons by different kings. They are not always in use, and they can each hold only a few of the more dangerous prisoners at a time. These seem like the most promising prospects, in my opinion. The fewer ears to hear, the better."

Studying the map, Letty followed a path from the farthest prison back to the castle. The trail snaked its way through mountains and woods, branching off at each of the three prisons. As it approached the castle, it entered the dark forest. The pale yellowish color of the paper contrasted with the inky-black grouping of trees, and as she saw that the path sliced through the forest, Letty's heart seized in her chest. "Ummm . . . we're going to go through the dark forest?"

Princess Maisy looked grim. Everyone in the kingdom had been taught the dangers of the dark forest from the time they were very young, the princess included. Not noticing Letty's wariness, the princess casually continued, "Yes, it's an unfortunate obstacle, but it can't be helped. Surely we can figure out the forest's mysteries and overcome them."

Letty fought the fear taking hold of her, not wanting her nerves to be noticed by her friend, who had not stopped speaking.

Princess Maisy rested her finger on the last of the three prisons, set high on top of what appeared to be a small mountain. "I really think this is the one. It's just too perfect. There would be no casual travelers passing by because it's so isolated, which makes it ideal for hiding Uncle Henrick's schemes. It is also a tall tower with a small prison room at the top that can only hold two prisoners, which is probably why Uncle Henrick hasn't transported your father and Rylan there; it's already full. I don't think the other two prisons are even staffed regularly."

"That all makes sense, but is there no way we can go around the dark forest?" Letty asked again in a small voice.

Princess Maisy shook her head. "No, I think it will add too much time to the trip, and we need to hurry. The winter storms are coming fast, and there aren't many towns in the area. The less marching through the countryside we can do, the better." She started rolling up the maps while she talked, then finally noticed Letty's nervous expression. Her voice softened. "It would be nice to have a decent hunter with us, but at least your father taught your brother how to get by in the wilderness, and I've also had many lessons in archery, which I can honestly say I'm quite good at. So I should be able to hunt for us, with your brother's navigating help. I believe it is perfectly plausible for us to get there and back with few issues," the princess finished with a bright grin and confident toss of her head as she attempted to console Letty.

Knowing the princess may not understand how treacherous the journey could be, Letty began fidgeting with her dress. "Have you ever been in the dark forest?"

"No, but surely it's not so bad. Have you?"

"No, but I've heard many stories, and I'm sure you have, too. Is there really no way to go around?" Letty pleaded.

"We are hitting cold months. Your father and Rylan could be sent to another prison at any moment, which will complicate things further. We need to take the fastest route."

The logic was sound, but Letty was not thrilled with the prospect of wandering in the dark forest, and deep down, she was troubled.

Worried the captain might return at any moment, the girls

began putting the maps away until Letty had another thought. "Don't we need the maps?"

"No, I know the maps well enough, I shouldn't need to bring one with us. There's a chance my uncle could notice its absence." The princess's confidence was in full force now, and Letty could see that objecting would get her nowhere, but it felt to her like it might not be the best plan. After her family's experience on the mountain, Letty knew how quickly things could go badly in the wilderness. One moment, they were all healthy and hiking with a clear path in front of them. The next, Miles's ankle was broken and snow covered the path ahead, impeding their progress.

However, Princess Maisy seemed secure in her knowledge of the terrain, so Letty pushed the uneasy feeling aside and rolled up another parchment as she said, "I'll come back to put the books away after lunch. Let's get you dressed."

CHAPTER 17

Letty wanted to talk to Clement before going back to clean up the library, so she hurried through lunch and asked Elias, the stable boy, to relay a message for her. Elias ran off to the barracks, and Letty exited the back door, nodding to the guards and feigning a walk through the garden. As soon as she turned the corner of the castle, she moved into the pocket of trees Clement had shown her a few days prior.

The sun trickled through the trees, so no good shadows presented a hiding place for them to talk, which caused Letty to anxiously twist at her dress. Noticing her nerves, she focused on the sunlight and the few birds singing in the trees while she waited. After a few minutes, branches snapped behind her, and she turned to see Clement stepping through the trees.

"This needs to be the last time, Letty. This doesn't look good." He pulled a note from his pocket and placed it into her waiting hand. "That's what you needed. Please don't ask me for anything else. The captain is getting more strict by the day."

Letty looked at the note and, finding what she needed, slipped it into a small opening at the front of her dress. "I promise I won't bother you again. Thank you for everything, Clement. I won't forget it."

The large guard shook his head as he moved away through the trees. "Be careful."

I'll do my best, she thought as she sneaked back through the trees to the garden path and rushed to tidy the library. As she stepped through the large oak doors into the red-carpeted room, she was met again with beautiful sunlight. Yellow beams reached through the glass windows, revealing flurries of dust, and wherever the light touched the carpet, the crimson color transformed to a shocking cherry red. Letty was glad to enjoy the room to herself for once, and she happily set to the task of putting books away.

Because of her sling, work was slow. She carried books from the map table at the back of the room and returned them to their homes on the shelves. As she grabbed three books and headed to the "A" section, she turned a little too fast and caught her foot on the carpet. The books flew out of her hands as she desperately tried to stop herself from falling and further injuring her shoulder. After a few quick steps, she steadied herself with a sigh of relief. Looking around on the floor, she located the first two dropped books, but the last was nowhere to be seen. Awkwardly, she lowered herself onto her three usable limbs and crawled around the carpet while looking for the escapee, spotting it deep under the map table. Sighing, she wedged herself between the large, elegantly sculpted legs of the massive table. The book was still out of reach, and she found herself wriggling like a worm to protect her shoulder but still reach the book. She giggled, thinking of how ridiculous she must look and how glad she was that no one else was in the room. Right as she grasped the troublesome book, she heard a loud thud!

Startled, Letty smacked her head against one of the legs, but in her current position, she couldn't do anything other than inch backward, ignoring the throbbing pain on the back of her skull and wondering what had made the noise. As she stood, she found herself face-to-face with Captain Foust.

His deep voice rumbled through the library, and she noticed his mustache bouncing up and down as he spoke. The strip of facial hair was so tremendously fuzzy that she couldn't see his mouth moving. In any other circumstance, Letty would have found it quite humorous, but her head ached, and a feeling of dread coursed through her body.

"Miss Letty," he said as he plucked the book out of her hand. "I have looked forward to meeting you since your return to the castle. I am intrigued to meet the little servant who has caused so many issues for the king, but it would appear Princess Maisy takes up most of your time." He plopped the book onto the table before looking at her expectantly.

"It is my job to take care of the princess and ensure her needs are met. I was just cleaning up from her study session."

"Hmmmm." He placed both hands behind his back, his stance stiff as he began a lap around the large oak table. "I do not believe you, Miss Letty."

Struggling to keep her voice steady, Letty said, "I don't know why not. It is my job to clean up after the princess, which is what I'm doing."

Captain Foust stopped just behind her and leaned forward. She froze in place. "Miss Letty, you have caused nothing but trouble for our great king since your arrival. If I say I do not believe you, I have reason to." He continued his walk around the table. "I know all about your visits to the dungeon, though I've yet to determine why you visited. The guard was quite tight-lipped during his interrogation."

"You interrogated him? Why?" It was difficult to hear that Lewis's dismissal had been even more traumatic than she had imagined. "Lewis did nothing wrong. Princess Maisy had commanded me to take food and blankets to the prisoners. He simply followed orders. He didn't deserve to lose his position."

"That is my decision to make, and I am always right with regard to my men. But you . . ." He paused and looked at her. "You see, Miss Letty, Princess Maisy should not have known about those prisoners in the first place."

"This is her castle. This is her kingdom. Why shouldn't she know that men are in her dungeon?"

The mustache tilted up slightly on one side. Letty thought the captain might actually be smiling. "That is interesting. Last I checked, the ruler of this kingdom is currently named King Henrick. NOT Princess Maisy. I could have you arrested for treason." He strolled around the far side of the table. "Are these some of the stories you have been spewing to the princess to give her such a strong will? We did not have issues with her until you arrived."

Letty stood tall as she said boldly, "Princess Maisy has done nothing wrong."

"Maybe not, but we're not talking about her. The question is, what have you done wrong? Why were you just snooping around the library?"

"I was not snooping. I was picking up books that I dropped."
She lifted her sling to show why she was so clumsy. "It's not easy
carrying stacks of books with one hand."

"Hmmmm . . ." He was pacing back around the table behind
her as he said, "I have learned very little from this visit, but what I
do know is that you are up to something, Miss Letty, and I do not
like it. Be careful where you snoop in the future. I'd hate to throw
you in the dungeon with your two friends."

Chills ran through Letty's spine, and she fought the urge to
recoil from Captain Foust's clear threat, but instead, she picked up
a pile of books and turned to put them away. "Please allow me to
do my job. I'm already running behind."

Captain Foust chuckled, and his mustache hopped up and
down. "Yes, Miss Letty, please return to your duties. My apologies
for interrupting you, but do listen to my words. Things are about
to change."

Moving like a rigid stick across the room, Captain Foust reached
the door, turned abruptly, and removed his hat in one swift
motion. His mustache curled up on one side as he gave Letty a
grand bow, the feather of his hat making a wide arc through the air
above him. "I expect to see you again soon in much more dire
circumstances. I wish you the best of luck."

As the door shut behind him, Letty sank to the floor, shock and
fear on her face. Princess Maisy was right: Captain Foust was not a
nice man.

CHAPTER 18

Shoving one dress after another aside, Letty attempted to find something remotely appropriate for journeying across the kingdom, but Princess Maisy's wardrobe was created for beauty, not function. Since her encounter with Captain Foust in the library, Letty's initial fear had transformed into determination. The captain had tried to stop her with his threats, but those same threats showed her how far the kingdom had plummeted into cruelty, corruption, and injustice. Their plans seemed more important now than ever.

Pushing aside an exquisite dress, Letty snatched its hanger from the armoire. "Your Highness, do you by chance have something else more suitable for travel in the wilderness?" She held up a silken black gown with hints of lavender peeking through the ruffled skirt that swept the floor. "From experience, this is not something I would want to hike in."

Princess Maisy chuckled as she set her book down. "You're right. That simply will not do. Where is the dress I attempted to wear on my walk with the prince? The laundress must have put it around here somewhere."

Letty replaced the dress she used for emphasis and searched unsuccessfully among the folds of skirts crowding the bottom of the armoire. With a sigh, she closed the doors, wondering if the seamstress could make a new traveling outfit in the morning without raising any suspicions.

Though Letty had been frightened by her encounter with Captain Foust, she quickly realized that they couldn't back down now, despite his threats. If anything, the confrontation had made her more determined than ever. She knew that something must be done to return justice and integrity to Trielle.

As she pondered, her eye fell on a large chest huddled in the far corner of the room. It was as tall as her waist, with elaborately carved trumpet vines and flowers trailing up the sides and over the edges. The corners were covered in tarnishing metal that must have shone brightly once, but the chest now looked old and neglected. She had never looked in there, or really even paid attention to it at all, but several capes lay on top of it, so perhaps the more practical clothes had been stored in the chest, out of sight. She moved over to the chest, removed the capes, and undid the latch.

The hinges on the lid protested loudly as Letty lifted. There was no clothing inside, but an assortment of old books, toys, and other dusty items met her gaze. As she reached to pick one up, she was startled by a gasp behind her.

"Letty, what do you think you're doing?!" Princess Maisy said in a choked voice.

Letty yelped in surprise, and the chest banged shut. "I . . . I was just trying to find some simpler clothes for you to wear. I thought perhaps there would be some in here."

"That chest belonged to my mother. When she died, her handmaid told me to store it in my room and keep it safe. I don't even think anybody remembers it's here anymore." Sadness tinted the princess's words as her voice grew quiet. "I've never opened it."

"Oh my," Letty whispered. "I am sorry, Your Highness."

Dismissing her glistening eyes with a wave, the princess said, "It's fine. I'm almost a grown woman who will someday rule a kingdom. I should be over such sentimental things by now."

Letty rushed to her side. "No, princess, of course not! This is your family! Your parents loved you, and I know they would love to see the kind and generous person you have become. Anything that ties them to you is a priceless treasure. I don't know what that chest holds, but maybe one day you will feel ready to open it and see what things were precious to your mother."

Princess Maisy hugged Letty in thanks. Wiping her eyes, she said, "You know, I feel stronger and more capable than ever. I haven't given a thought to that chest for a long time, but I do think I may be ready to open it—since you have so generously tested it out already," the princess teased.

"Oh, Princess Maisy, I didn't mean to impose, and I don't want to force you to do anything you're not ready to do. This might be really hard."

The princess stood and reached out her hand. "With a friend like you by my side, I know I can face hard things," she said with a gentle smile.

Letty smiled back as she took the princess's hand and walked toward the chest. Together, they lifted the lid all the way up so it stayed propped open, despite the squeaking hinges. A musty smell hit their noses, and then both jaws dropped as their eyes quickly surveyed the contents that had been stowed away for so many years.

The chest was filled with a variety of things. On top, they caught sight of the old books Letty had noticed before. When they picked them up, they saw that these leather-bound books were all about botany, and there were dozens of pressed flowers scattered throughout the pages.

"I adore flowers, Your Highness, and it looks like your mother did, too," Letty sighed.

Princess Maisy gingerly flipped through a volume, stroking the dried petals. "Isn't that interesting? The two people who have cared for me and taught me more than anyone else both love flowers—fragile, beautiful things." She picked up a dried violet and twisted it between her fingers. "I think flowers are wonderful, too, but I would say my favorite part of nature is birds. I always wish my garden had more birds."

Returning the flower to the pages, the princess continued browsing the chest with glistening eyes and came across a pair of brand-new work gloves. "My father used to lovingly scold my mother when she came into the castle covered in soil. Her beautiful hands would often have dirt nestled under her fingernails, and I know my father secretly loved her more for it. I have very few memories of my parents, but most of them involve the garden. I remember walking outside with my mother every day. She loved wearing her hair down, and whenever she bent over to smell a blossom, the bright colors would contrast beautifully with her black hair." She sniffled as she spoke. "Those are some of my clearest memories of them—Father laughing and scolding her for getting dirty and Mother walking with me in the garden."

"Those are beautiful memories. I'm so sorry, Your Highness."

Princess Maisy shook her head. "It was a long time ago. It's sad, but it also feels very good to let myself remember."

The girls continued to inspect the chest, finding some of Princess Maisy's baby toys and shoes, a portrait of the queen as a little girl, and a tiny tiara among the treasures. Letty was wrong for thinking there were no clothes in the chest; tucked into protective boxes were fabric masterpieces covered in precious jewels.

"The dresses are magnificent, Your Highness. She was petite like you, and if you like any, I could have them cleaned."

Princess Maisy's hair bobbed up and down as she nodded. Letty lifted a deep red gown with lace accents and a sparkling skirt that must have been glorious in a candlelit ballroom. She shook it out to show the princess. As she flicked the dress, a small scroll came tumbling out of the folds and rolled to the princess's feet.

"What's that?" Letty asked.

Princess Maisy tilted her head as she picked up the little scroll. "It has my parents' seal."

Curiously, the girls inspected the scroll, but since it was sealed, they couldn't read it. Letty retrieved a letter opener from the writing desk, handing it to the princess.

The small knife scraped gingerly against the paper breaking the wax seal. As careful fingers unrolled the yellowing scroll, both girls held their breath. At full length, the paper was about ten inches long, and Letty could see the beautiful handwritten script, but it was too small and far away for her to read along. Letty watched Princess Maisy's eyes grow large as she read. Then her face suddenly turned to stone, and she stood abruptly. "Get my tiara, Letty. My official one. I am paying a visit to Uncle Henrick."

Letty sat dumbfounded. "But—but what is it, Your Highness?"

Princess Maisy moved behind the dressing screen. "With haste! Please!"

Jumping to her feet, Letty scrambled to find the tiara as Princess Maisy slid into a magnificent purple dress. "This scroll is a royal decree written by my parents and witnessed by my uncle. I was supposed to inherit this kingdom nearly two years ago. Not at twenty-one years of age. At sixteen."

Letty's mouth dropped open. "You're supposed to be the queen? Right now?"

"Yes! And as queen, I can free your father and the cobbler. I can bring the mapmaker and his son home! Now get my tiara!"

The large box with the tiara nearly fell on Letty's head in her haste, but she caught it and placed it in front of the princess, who motioned to the back of her dress. "Button me up quickly, please." She flicked open the box and placed the sparkling tiara on her head, throwing her shoulders back and standing tall and proud in front of the mirror. The small scroll was gripped in one hand as she swung open the door and marched down the hall with Letty following.

Moonlight trickled through the windows and, with most of the castle sleeping, the girls' footsteps echoed eerily through the silent hallways. The princess moved with determination. As they turned the last corner to descend the staircase, Letty was dismayed to see the tall, feathered hat and piercing eyes of the captain of the guard. Her stomach dropped as he said, "Your Highness, what are you doing up at this time of night? You should be resting." His eyes narrowed as they met Letty's, but she held her ground as Princess Maisy spoke.

"I must speak to Uncle Henrick immediately."

"I believe you meant to say King Henrick, Your Highness."

The princess looked glorious as she lifted her chin up high. Moonlight hit the tiara just right, scattering tiny specks of light on the walls around them. "I mean Uncle Henrick. Please move out of my way."

Captain Foust's jaw set tightly as he looked from Princess Maisy to Letty and back again. "What is in your hand, Your Highness?" He reached for the scroll as Princess Maisy yanked her hand away.

"It is for Uncle Henrick's eyes only."

He cooly replied, "Well, we have a new procedure. As captain of the guard, any business for the king must first go through me." With that, his hand whipped out and snatched the scroll from Princess Maisy's hand.

Letty gasped, but the princess remained composed as an icy fury swept over her features. "How *dare* you?"

Ignoring the two girls, Captain Foust stepped to the side to read the scroll by a stream of moonlight. "Interesting." His eyes met Letty's. "I assume this is all your doing. I believe the king has had quite enough of you." Rolling the scroll up and pocketing it, he raised a single finger, and two guards appeared. "You will return to your room and stay there for the foreseeable future, Your Highness. As for Miss Letty," he said through clenched teeth, "pack your bags. You will no longer be in Princess Maisy's service."

Looking from Letty to Captain Foust, Princess Maisy calmly stated, "You have no right to relieve my lady-in-waiting, and you have no right to take my property. As you have just read, I am the rightful ruler of Trielle at this time. Return the scroll to me at once." Letty saw the corner of her mouth twitch; though the princess was putting on a brave face, Letty could see that she was scared.

Captain Foust stiffened even more. His words were coated in rage and came out like a growl: "Go ahead and try to prove it, Your Highness. You have nothing to go on without this scroll. It is my duty to protect King Henrick and his throne. Now return to your room before I call the guards to escort Miss Letty to the dungeon."

Letty realized how mistaken they had been to come with the scroll that would remove King Henrick from the throne. Of course he would never allow it to be known. She knew the princess had realized the same thing: she had lost the only proof of her claim as queen. Letty's heart felt the enormity of the mistake, and she stood next to the princess, swallowing at the thought of the dungeon. The captain spun abruptly, his sharp footsteps echoing as he stormed away. "Guards, take them back to their rooms and see that they do not have any further episodes of sleepwalking. You will be leaving in the morning, Miss Letty. I will find another servant to assist you, Your Highness."

As they were marched back to their rooms, Princess Maisy put an arm around Letty and said in a seething whisper, "I guess it's decided. We're leaving tonight."

1.ONSP437-157883 Printed in USA Sep-2024